MAKING SWEDISH COUNTRY FURNITURE AND HOUSEHOLD THINGS

A Cloudburst Press Book

Published in the U.S.A. by
Hartley & Marks, Inc.
P.O. Box 147
Point Roberts, WA 98281

Published in Canada by
Hartley & Marks, Ltd.
3663 W. Broadway
Vancouver, B.C. V6R 2B8

Adapted for North American woodworkers by Ron Willick
Black and white photos: Sven Nilsson, except pp. 50, 59, 75, 78, 82, 101, 103, 107, 114, 118, 119, 149, 161, and 183, which were provided by the Nordic Museum; pp. 32, 37, 93, 111, 152, and 153, by Olle Ekberg; p. 92 by Eva Sjöberg; and p. 92 by Hans Keijser. The newly made furniture on pp. 32, 93, 127, 151, and 174 was created by Tage Stilander, Östervåla Handicrafts; the rest were made by Bengt and Lars Sjöberg. Technical drawings by Sia Kaskamanidis and Bob English.

Library of Congress Cataloging-in-Publication Data

Keijser, Hans.
[Snickra möbler och bruksting efter gamla svenska förebilder. English]
Making Swedish country furniture and household things / Hans Keijser and Lars Sjöberg.
p. cm.
Translation of: Snickra möbler och bruksting efter gamla svenska förebilder.
"A Cloudburst Press book."
Includes bibliographical references.
ISBN 0-88179-023-0 (alk. paper) : $12.95 ($14.95 Can.)
1. Furniture making. 2. Country furniture--Sweden. I. Sjöberg, Lars, 1941- . II. Title.
TT194.K4513 1989
684.104'09485--dc20 89-39404
CIP

First Swedish edition 1976

Designed and typeset by The Typeworks
Manufactured in the United States of America
Printed on acid-free paper
1st Printing, 1990

MAKING SWEDISH COUNTRY FURNITURE AND HOUSEHOLD THINGS

Hans Keijser

Lars Sjöberg

ADAPTED BY *Ron Willick*

A Cloudburst Press Book

Hartley & Marks

CONTENTS

INTRODUCTION

FURNITURE

CONTENTS

CONTENTS

INTRODUCTION

MAKING COUNTRY FURNITURE FROM OLD SWEDISH MODELS

This book has two goals. The first is to share an exceptionally fine tradition of functional furniture and household items made with wood. These everyday items come from every social stratum, and their common denominator is their functional form and timeless design. Unfortunately, it was often precisely such objects that were worn out by assiduous use over decades and centuries, and then discarded because they were considered too ordinary to preserve. They have become so rare, even though they were once the most common of all, that people have totally forgotten about them in favor of antique fine furniture and luxury articles.

The other goal is to pass on to everyone who will ever work with wood—both amateur and professional cabinetmakers—the partially interrupted tradition of craftsmanship associated with handicraft production.

All the original pieces were accurately measured and drawn full size, and these drawings were then reduced. Certain details, however, have been reproduced in 1:1 scale. Of course, anyone wishing to have 1:1 scale drawings can enlarge them.

It should be pointed out that the models in the book are individual examples and that obviously there were variations in proportions and detailing. Gate-legged tables, for instance, were made in many sizes, and the models varied according to their place of origin and the craftsman. Within any one historical period, however, there were certain common general guidelines for table and chair heights.

For this reason, each woodworker should feel free to change proportions and dimensions according to his or her own needs. Nevertheless, in this book, our ambition has been to reproduce the appearance of each piece of furniture or household item as closely as possible. In this way we avoid the risk of adapting the shapes, consciously or not, to contemporary ideals of style, which might result in their becoming "dated" more quickly. Furthermore, since most of the examples in the book are without stylistic decoration, we hope that they will be accepted not only as catalysts for design solutions but aslo as actual design models. Much from the past still fulfills its original function in contemporary life, despite the fact that the environment has changed dramatically. We hope that at least some of the things in this book will awaken interest in the language of form in olden times and in the Swedish woodworking tradition.

Using the models in the book, we recommend that you make the necessary working drawings (for instance, for the completion of dining-room chairs or the like) so as to obtain usable furniture and household items. In general we suggest that it is safest to follow the proportions, details, materials, etc., of the models as faithfully as possible, since these were all generally determined by durability and utility.

WOOD

The objects described in this book were constructed primarily of pine or hardwood, usually alder or birch. Pine was used for the simpler types of furniture and household items, such as the gate-legged table, the shelves, the hanging cabinet, the clothes rack, the flour box, and the cutting boards. Alder or birch were used for the heavier furniture and decorative objects, or for furniture that was to be decorated with profiles or cutouts, such as the stepladder, the armchair, the ornament shelf, and the six-armed chandelier.

When buying wood it is not necessary to select the best, clearest quality wood; a lesser quality is fine as long as all the knots are firmly seated. Since in the past most furniture was painted, a cross-grained knot was acceptable in a chair frame or tabletop. The knot was visible underneath the paint (putty was not used). Accepting wood with all its irregularities is certainly something we should take up again.

The measurements of the objects in the book are often but not always adjusted to today's standardized lumber yard dimensions. Sometimes they may just match by accident.

In some places it might be difficult to get hold of wood dry enough for cabinet work. At lumber yards and building supply stores there is often only pine to be had, and this lumber contains far too much moisture to be used right away. It should be kiln dried or stored at a warm room temperature for at least two to three months before it is used. During the drying period the wood must be stored with stickers between each layer of planks so that the air has a chance to circulate. It is sawed or planed to standard dimensions and sold in the following dimensions: 1″ × 2″, 1″ × 4″, 1″ × 6″, 1″ × 8″—up to 1″ × 12″. And as 2″ × 2″, 2″ × 4″, 2″ × 6″ — up to 2″ × 12″. Planed 1″ lumber is actually ¾″ thick, while planed 2″ lumber is actually 1½″ thick. For dry lumber, all width dimensions will be ½″ less once they have been planed. For example, a dry planed 2″ × 6″ board actually measures 1½″ × 5½″.

Lumber purchased from a hardwood supplier is rough sawn and can be planed to your specifications. Since lumber from a hardwood supplier is kiln or air dried, it should be stored in a dry area. Hardwood suppliers can usually provide furniture grade hardwoods and softwoods. They can be found under the heading Hardwoods in the Yellow Pages. If all your lumber is not dry, checking, warpage, and shrinkage will occur.

If you have access to a commercial cabinet maker in your area, they may be willing to sell you dry pine and hardwood.

In the past, a tabletop was composed of two or three wide boards. The quality of the wood, combined with the long, careful drying it had to undergo, meant that even large tabletops seldom warped. Now we have to be content with butt jointed panels, which can be ordered at the cabinet factory and are used for tabletops, chair seats, chest lids, etc. These panels consist of glued-together boards, approximately 2–3″ wide. Before gluing to the desired panel size, the boards are turned so that the annual rings are opposite each other, but with the core side always in the same direction. In this way the panel is prevented from warping. (Using glued matched boards as a replacement for butt jointed slabs is not recommended, since this type of panel will warp.) One important detail to remember about butt jointed panels is that you have to plane the panels yourself to the finished thickness. It will then be a fine surface with traces of the plane. The factory's thickness planer or sander, on the other hand, will make the slab look just as even as plywood.

A cabinet factory can also help you with splitting wood from thick dimensions to those more suitable for your project. Make the most of wood that you have cut down in your own yard. Apple and pear trees that have been sawed into planks and allowed to dry sufficiently are perfectly suited for woodworking.

TRADITIONAL TOOLS

Making simple household items and furniture before the days of electric machines was not as different from the way we work today as you might think. Many tools and methods have an ancient tradition, but a lot of the old knowledge has been forgotten, especially during the past few decades. Getting to know primitive or old-fashioned hand tools, and learning to work with them, does not have to be a flight from the reality of the labor-saving machines of today. Understanding and applying working methods handed down for generations, and using tools of simple design, is more likely to make woodworking easier for you than to make it more difficult.

Simple traditional hand tools can still be bought. They are made with wood, but the wood is being replaced more and more by steel or plastic. Such tools may sometimes be hard to get hold of. In most hardware stores, both in small towns and big cities, they are generally not stocked because of

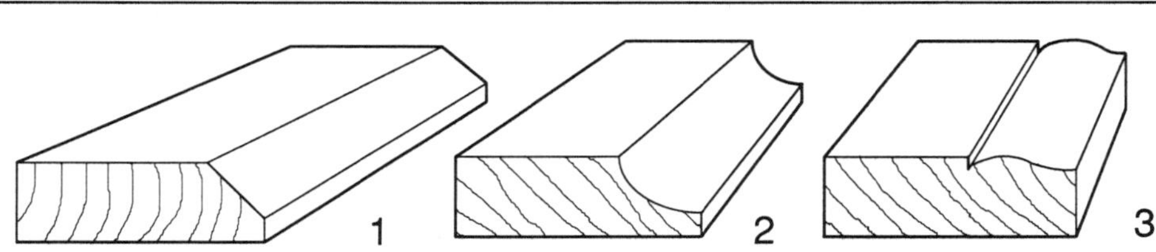

1. Chamfer, made with a chamfer plane. See the bottom of the chest, page 135. (When a chamfer plane is unavailable, a block plane run across a corner works quite nicely.)
2. Fluting, made with molding plane, or with a router, for the non-purist. See the hollow molding of the hanging cabinet, page 143.
3. Profile, made with a profile plane, molding plane, shaper, or router. See the edging of the stepladder, page 57.

the small demand. However, they can be ordered by mail from woodworking tool suppliers which advertise in such woodworking magazines as Fine Woodworking, American Woodworking, and others.

Profile or molding planes are no longer available in stores. They are only found at auctions or at some old cabinetmakers who are willing to lend them out. Cabinet shops usually have a grinder, and for a fee can grind a blade to the correct profile and mill the quantity desired. Or you can try a machine shop or saw sharpening shop. Better frame shops and building supply stores may have a variety of moldings that can sometimes be used for mirror frames. (Moldings can also be made with a router or shaper. The bits and knives for these could also be made.)

When the pieces in this book were originally made there was not the same demand for perfection as there is today. A hundred years of industrialization has made us believe that the best and most beautiful things are those that are made in factories. Before, when everything was made by hand, of course it was all made as well as possible, but the eye was more tolerant and would accept, for instance, that the dimensions of a set of chairs did not match to a fraction of an inch. Furthermore, tool marks were quite acceptable in the objects that were made. Today we have far too much love for sandpaper, which results in the clarity of a profile or shape being sanded away.

JOINTS

In the past there were a few simple joints that remain with us today. Chests, boxes, and shelves were joined at the outer corners by a dovetail joint (see #8), which may sometimes be locked by wooden pegs.

Simpler shelves can be put together with rabbet joints (see #6), and wooden pegs. (See the Small Wall Shelf, page 89.)

Half-rabbet, or half-dado (see #1B) and dovetailed dado joints (see #2) are used to join shelves with shelf sides. Half-dovetail joints (see #3) with a slanting tenon piece are used for stools. Dovetail joints (see #4) are used for the dovetail bracing strips in tabletops. Large tabletops, such as that of the gate-legged table, are strengthened and held together by dovetail bracing strips. The bracing strip always goes across the grain of the slab. On the underside of the tops, dovetail grooves are made from the hinge side to approximately 2″ inside the outer edges. The profiled dovetail bracing strips are inserted but should only be glued at one point, by the hinge side, to prevent checking in the top. Note that the length of the dovetail groove must be longer than the dovetail bracing strips so that the slab can move in reaction to the humidity in the air.

All doweled tenon joints (see #9) made in chair or table legs, or lid frames, are always locked with one or two wooden dowels. Wooden dowels are also used to fasten moldings, bottoms, and the backs of chests and cabinets, for example. Doweling or pinning a tenon in a lid frame is done by first making the dowel and fitting it into the corresponding tap-hole, then drilling one or two holes completely or almost completely through the frame and the tenon. The wooden dowels can be shaped from pine to fit snugly, or dowels of the correct diameter may be used. The dowels must not be carved too large or else they can crack the piece. If carved too small they will not

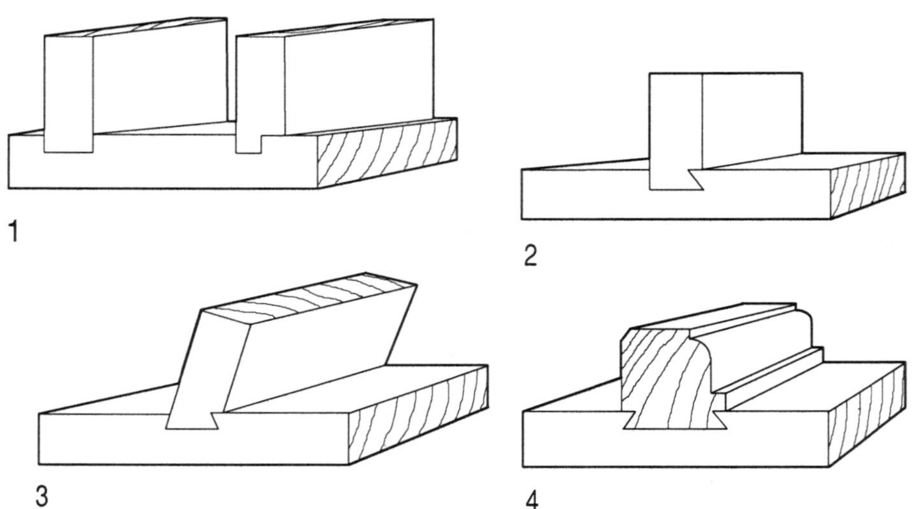

1. Dadoed joint. Used for fastening the middle shelf of the Small Wall Shelf to the shelf sides.
   Half-rabbet joint which is used for fastening shelves into shelf sides.
2. Dovetailed dado joint. Used for fastening shelves into shelf sides.
3. Angled dovetailed dado joint with slanting tenon. Used to fasten the leg sides of the stools to the seat.
4. Sliding dovetailed dado joint. Used to fasten the dovetail bracing strips to the top of the Gate-legged Table.
5. Groove slot, made with a router. See the lid frame of the Hanging Cabinet.

lock the construction sufficiently and may fall out of the hole. If any of the dowels hit bottom and stick out, cut off the projecting piece with a chisel.

Carved locking pins with a head are used to fasten a tabletop to its frame. (See the Gate-legged Table and the Trestle Table.)

A round tenon will work as a hinge for a lid, for instance, if it is carved out of the lid material and allowed to project into holes made in the side pieces. (See the Box with Lid.)

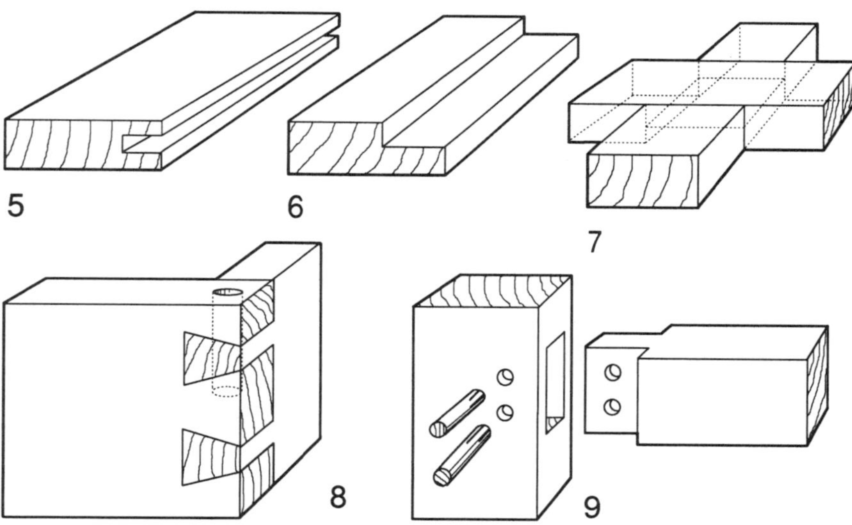

6. Rabbet, made with a rabbet plane or table saw. See the Small Wall Shelf.
7. Half lap. Used for the foot cross of the Clothes Rack and the Four-armed Chandelier.
8. Dovetail joint, locked by wooden dowels. See the Chest.
9. Doweled tenon joint, locked by wooden dowels.

Note: Always cut pieces slightly larger than the given dimensions to allow for planing and chiseling joints.

Another way to fasten a tenon is by wedging. Note that the wedge must be placed perpendicular to the grain in the piece the tenon is to be fastened in, otherwise the wooden piece can crack. (See the Clothes Rack.)

The wedge can also be used to hold together furniture such as the Trestle Table and Trestle Bed. However, make sure that the wedges are not made too wide, or they will crack off the projecting tenons when they are pounded down.

The glue used in the past was a type of animal bone glue that was applied hot. The glue hardened and became brittle, and with time it pulverized and disappeared from the joints. Thanks to the wooden dowels the objects are still holding together. Now we have had plastic-based glue for over twenty years; it is easy to work with and creates strong joints, but we do not know how it will age. Even if we can rely on the strength of the glue, we should not eliminate the wooden dowels. They are important to the appearance, and they are practical. When you are fitting together or gluing a chair, the wooden dowels help to hold the working pieces together, and you avoid the space required by, and the expense of, clamps.

FITTINGS

Some of the objects in the book have fittings that were originally forged by hand. Such fittings can sometimes be obtained from a locksmith or a metalsmith who can work from a drawing. For example, it is important for the Chest to have the right type of hinges, as they belong to its decorative appeal. On the other hand, modern substitutes for most of the fittings are available commercially.

PAINTING AND STAINING

In the past most furniture received some sort of finish treatment, as it does today. The usual conception that peasant furniture was most often unpainted has proven to be incorrect, at least for the pieces we are concerned with here, from the 18th and 19th centuries. Only a few pieces of furniture were regarded as being so simple that they were not worth painting.

The most common method of finishing pieces of furniture was to paint them with an oil-based paint, consisting of powdered pigment mixed with boiled linseed oil and turpentine (about half of each, or in the proportion 2 parts turpentine to 1 part linseed oil). You can still do it this way. [Note: do not use raw linseed oil. Boiled linseed oil gives a hard surface, and the turpentine speeds up the drying process.]

Powdered pigments are available at many art supply stores. If you wish to exactly duplicate the original colors of the pieces in the book, you can do so by purchasing the pigments named in the how-to instructions. Both linseed oil and turpentine are widely available at hardware stores, paint stores, and art supply stores.

There are many advantages to mixing your own oil paints, compared with using pre-mixed base colors and tints. A simple mixture of zinc white and burnt green earth, for example, immediately gives the proper pearl-gray color, lighter or darker depending on the proportions used. The paint you mix yourself can be made moderately thin, so that it will not hide the piece's structure or fill in delicate moldings and ornamental carvings.

Before applying a coat of oil paint, to avoid uneven absorption by the wood, first apply, as a primer coat, a mixture of pure linseed oil and turpentine, about half each. When the surface is dry, sand it lightly, and then paint it with the linseed oil paint, preferably with a drying agent added, as it dries slowly. [Note: It is essential that the surface be quite dry before the next coat is applied. If you apply the primer thinly you will be able to better judge when it has dried than if it is thickly applied. If applied thickly it may appear dry but still be wet underneath.]

If you want to give your furniture an even more wear-resistant surface, for the third coat you can apply a thin protective layer of varnish, made from turpentine and linseed oil in the proportions 2:1. [Note: Be sure the second coat is perfectly dry before doing this. If your paint has not completely covered the wood, add a further coat when the previous ones are dry.] A traditional method for lending the surface a subtle sheen without its looking greasy was to rub the dried paint with horsehair or the like.

If you want to treat the surface of a newly made piece despite the fact that the original was never painted, we would only recommend applying (with a cloth, several applications) boiled linseed oil and turpentine, approximately 1 part linseed oil to 4 parts turpentine. We do not advise using any type of plastic-based varnish or plastic-based lacquer.

You should always avoid treating the surface of cutting boards, flour boxes, and other items used for the storage and preparation of food.

Besides oil paint, alcohol-based staining was another method of finishing the surface of furniture, particularly tables, bureaus, and similar pieces made of alder and oak from manor house and castles.

The varnish, a solution of shellac, alcohol, and possibly a pigment, was applied with a brush. Polishing the varnish afterwards became more common during the 19th century, when it became almost obligatory, especially for mahogany furniture.

PRIMING AND GILDING

All furniture has to be primed before gilding or pigmented varnishing. These are complicated techniques, difficult to achieve without long practice, and we suggest that you consult a professional for them. If there are no gilders in your vicinity, you might get help at a quality framing shop, which would be in contact with frame factories, or from a professional sign painter. For anyone who still would like to try these surface treatments, and as general information, we will give a brief description of the procedure here.

In gilding, the primer is a mixture of chalk powder (in Sweden, Malmö chalk), and a glue solution consisting of rabbit skin glue (available in powdered crystals) dissolved in hot water. The primer must sit in a hot-water bath during application so it will not set. It is brushed directly onto the wood. The wood is first roughed with sandpaper and coated once with only the plain glue solution. The primer is applied in several coats and must dry and set each time. (Plaster of Paris is often used where chalk powder is not available. The primer raises the grain of the wood so it can be sanded smooth. It also gives the wood a hard, smooth surface which causes the gold leaf to shine.)

Between each coat the surface must be sanded. The parts that are later to have gold leaf applied and then polished must first be treated with a special primer, which is made of only chalk, glue solution, and thinner. (Today, "fast drying gold size" is used as the primer.) When the priming is finished, the furniture can also be painted directly with a pigmented varnish. (I.e. gold or brass powder in a base of turpentine and linseed oil. This requires less surface preparation—just sealing and sanding the wood a few times.) The treatment continues with the application of gilding paste (gold size) to the surfaces to be polished to a shine. This is a mixture which in the past had a salmon or orange-red hue. During the 20th century the color has changed toward purplish-reddish brown. Gilding paste can also be yellow or green. The various colors lend the gilding a warm or cold hue.

The gilding paste is mixed with a glue dissolved in distilled water, together with the pigment. This mixture is brushed several times onto the places previously coated with a primer. The surfaces to have composition (imitation) gold leaf applied are brushed only with unpigmented glue. Composition gold leaf gives a matte finish.

In polishing gold leaf, a polishing stone on a shaft was used. These polishing stones are made of agate or bloodstone (hematite).

A simpler type of matte gilding is performed using so-called "gold size." This is a boiled linseed oil varnish, prepared so that 12–14 hours after application it has dried to a surface like adhesive tape, on which the gold leaf is placed.

As a finishing treatment, the composition gold leaf used to be coated with a matte or semi-matte varnish. In this way the gold was sealed and prevented from oxidizing.

MODERN ALTERNATIVES TO TRADITIONAL GOLD LEAF

Note: There are modern alternatives to these traditional gilding methods. Gold leaf kits are available from art supply stores, which also sell gold paint. Or, you can buy gold powder pigment to make your own paint. (Add the powder to a mixture of 2 parts turpentine and one part linseed oil.)

INSTRUCTIONS

1. Seal the wood with the plain glue mixture.
2. Sand off the raised grain.
3. Apply one coat of red gold size.
4. When it feels tacky, but not sticky, apply gold leaf to the gold size.
5. Burnish till smooth using the back of a spoon or a similar tool. Be sure to eliminate all air bubbles so the gold leaf will adhere completely and not flake off.
6. Do steps 3 to 5 in sections, since the gold leaf must be applied before the glue has completely dried.

REFERENCES

Mayer, Ralph, *The Artist's Handbook of Materials and Techniques,* Viking Press, NY, 1981.

O'Neil, Isabel, *The Art of the Painted Finish,* William Morrow & Co., NY, 1971.

TRAY AND CUTTING BOARDS

This tray for knives and forks is now in the kitchen wing of Skogaholm's manor house at Skansen, an open-air exhibition in Stockholm of historic buildings from all over Sweden. Trays like this were common in households during the 18th and 19th centuries and were used to store and carry tools or flatware with carbon steel blades, which had to be cleaned and sharpened after being washed. This tray has the usual shape with sloping sides. The wall between the compartments is raised in a bowed profile, and provides room for a sawed-out handle.

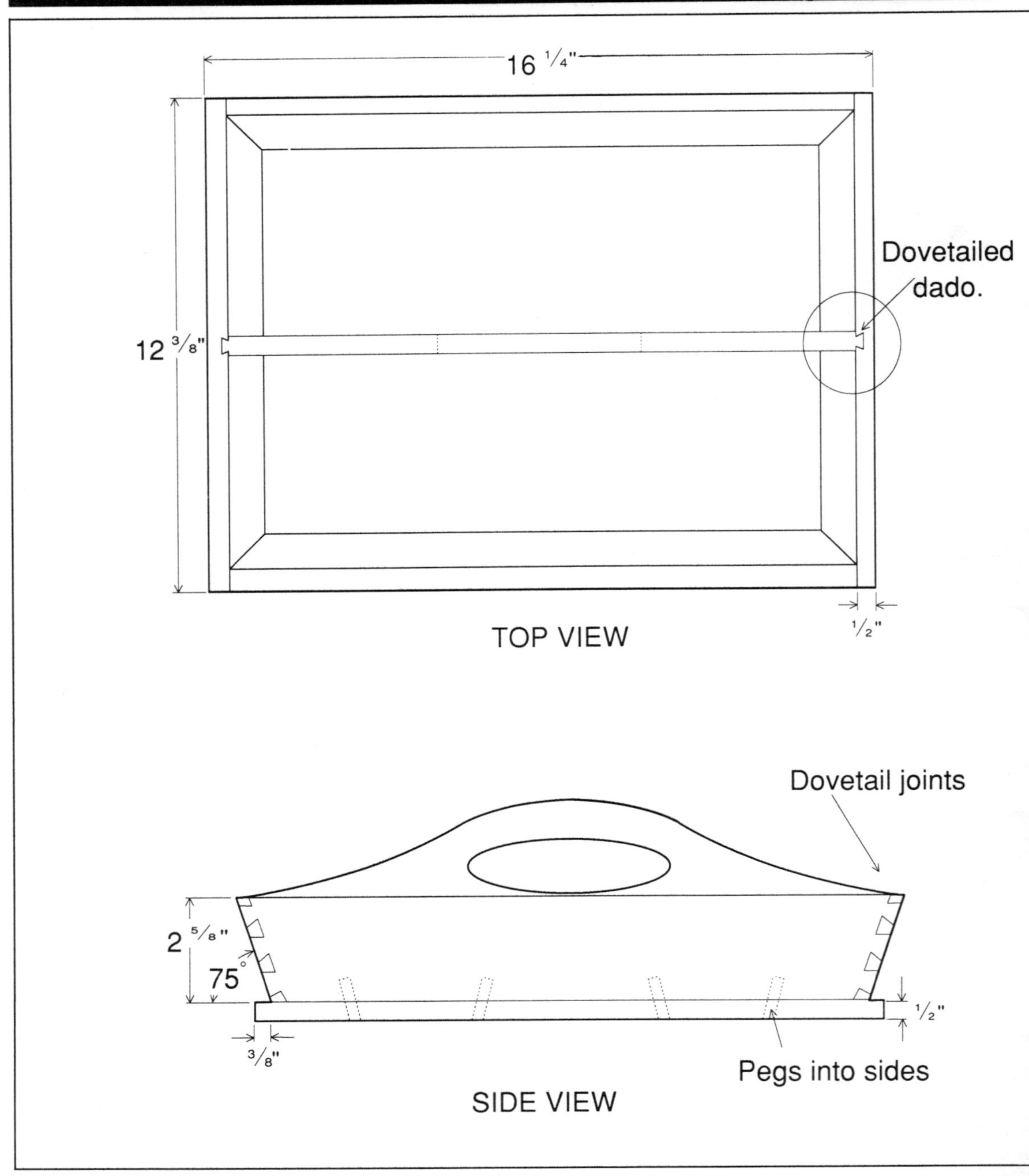

1/4" = 1
0 1 2 3 4 5 6 7 8 9 10 11 12

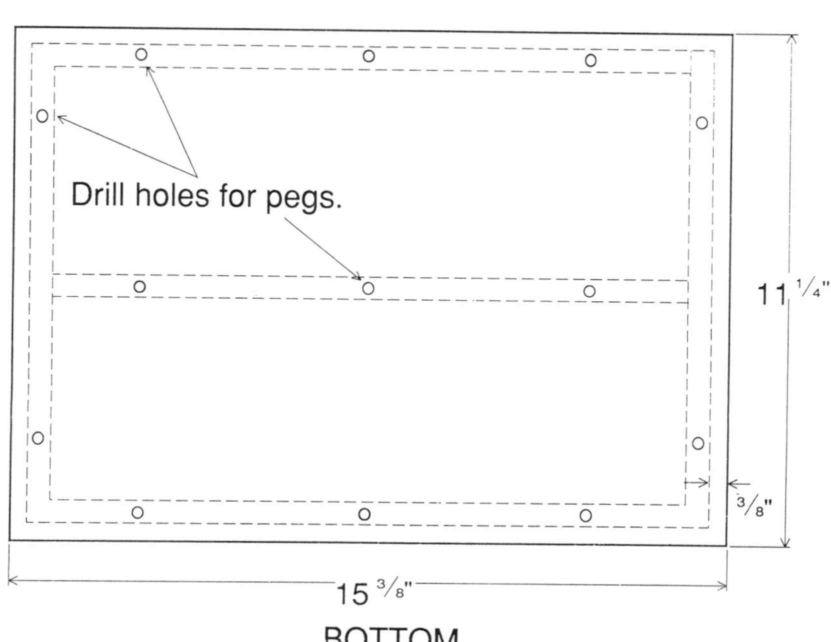
Drill holes for pegs.
11 1/4"
3/8"
15 3/8"
BOTTOM

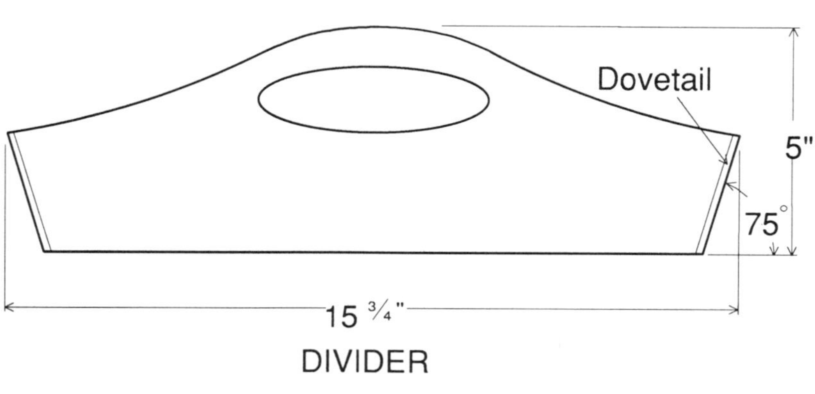
Dovetail
5"
75°
15 3/4"
DIVIDER

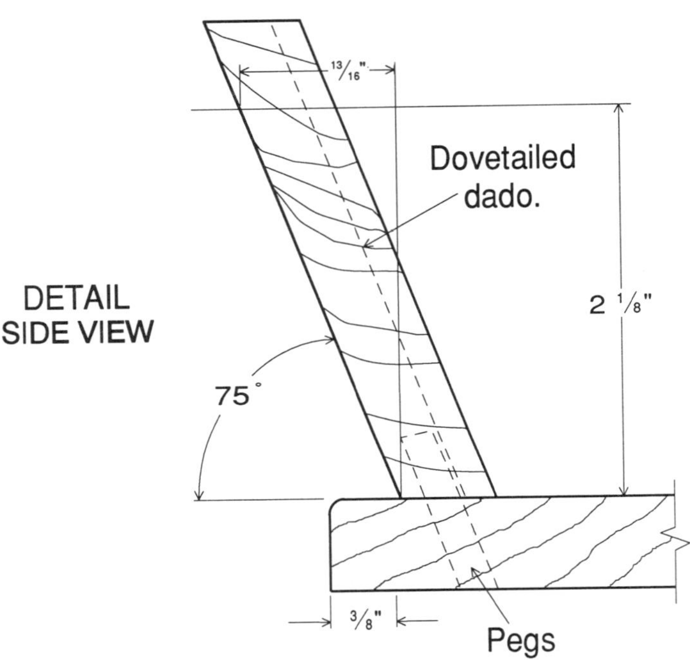

INSTRUCTIONS

Tray: Medium level of difficulty

Use pine, or a hardwood, such as oak to make this tray. Plane the sides and bottom to a thickness of ½″. Attach the sides with sliding dovetail joints (see Introduction, joint #4). Fasten the center wall to the short sides, also with joint #4. Fasten the bottom (which extends approximately ¼″ beyond the sides all the way around) to the sides with wooden pegs.

The tray may be brushed with a mixture of linseed oil and turpentine, or left unfinished.

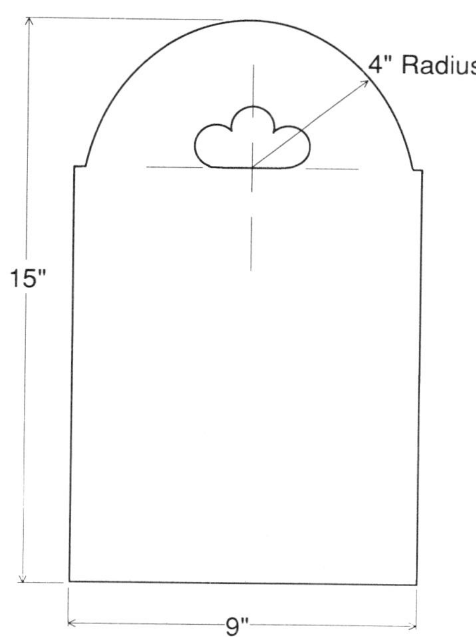

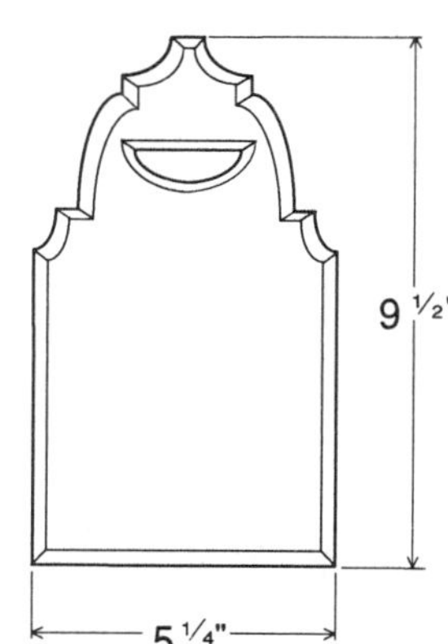

Here there are two examples of cutting boards, which in the past, as today, exhibited great variation in both shape and format. These two boards are also at the Skansen exhibit. The large one is in the kitchen wing of Skogaholm's manor house, and the small one in the kitchen of Delsbogården.

INSTRUCTIONS

Cutting Boards: Easy to make

Use birch to make the large cutting board. The thickness is planed to ¾″, the length is 15″, and the width is 9″. Make the shape of the hole by first boring three holes, and then shaping the edges with a wood chisel.

Use pine to make the small board. The thickness is planed to ½″, the length is 9½″, and the width is 5¼″. Contour the board and bevel the edges.

Leave the surface of both boards unfinished.

3/16" = 1 | 0 1 2 3 4 5 6 7 8 9 10 11 12 13 14 15 16

BOX WITH LID

This box is now in the kitchen wing in the Skogaholm manor house at the Skansen exhibit. It was originally intended to hold flour, oatmeal, salt, and the like, but it is easy to imagine many other uses. The format and detailing were varied to serve several purposes.

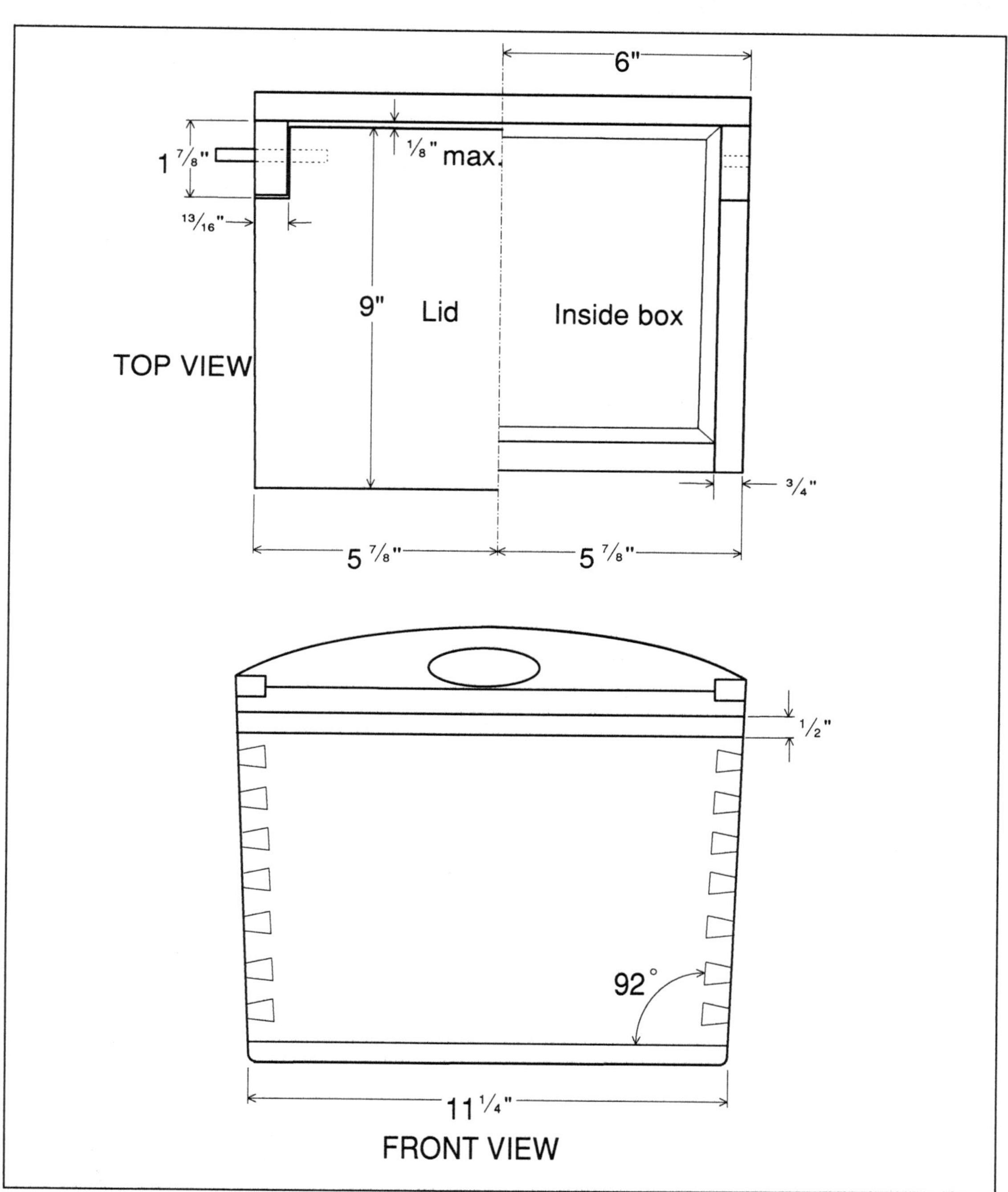
6"
1 7/8"
1/8" max.
13/16"
9"
Lid
Inside box
TOP VIEW
3/4"
5 7/8"
5 7/8"
1/2"
92°
11 1/4"
FRONT VIEW
0 1 2 3 4 5 6 7 8 9 10 11 12
1/4" = 1

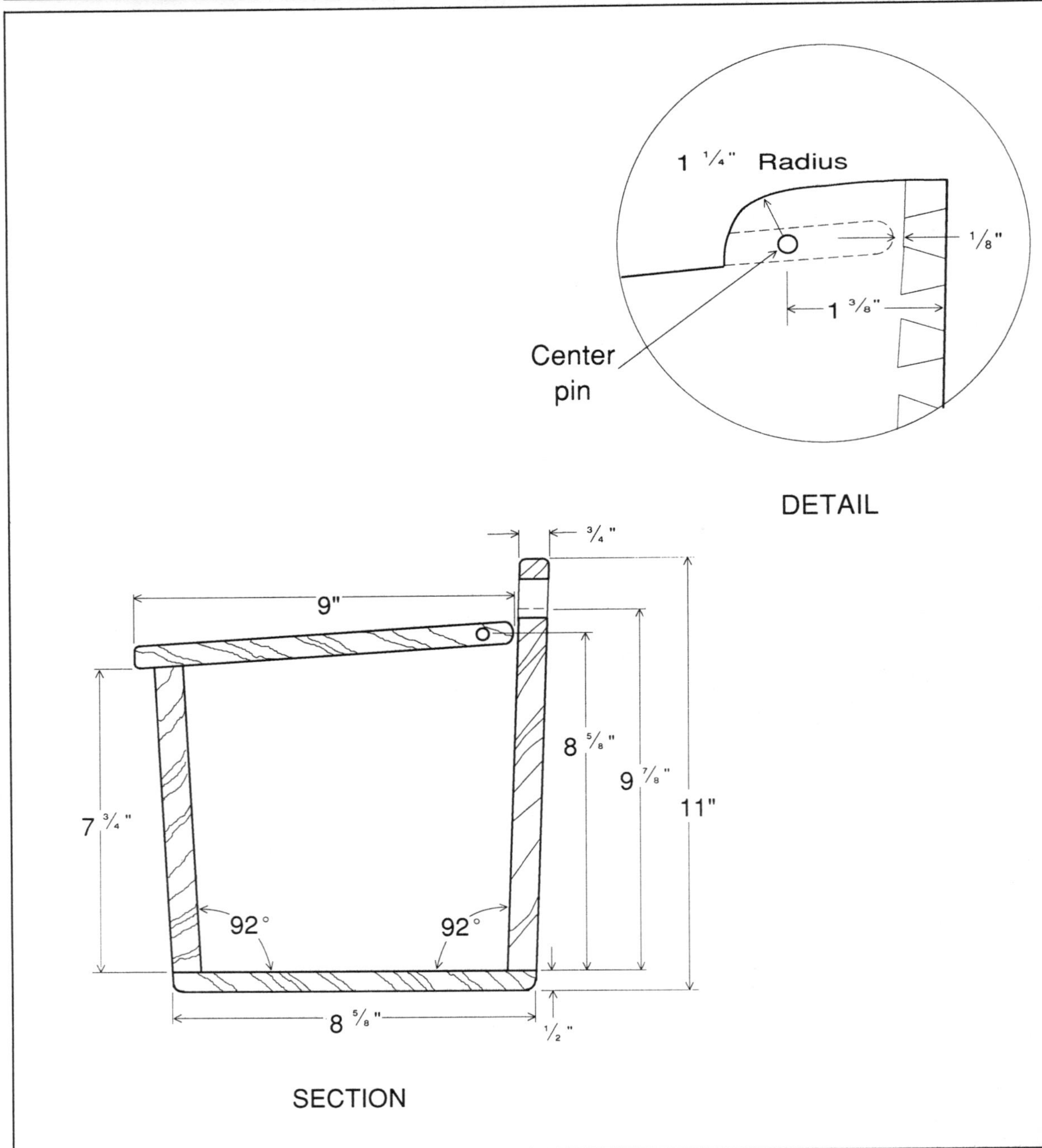

1/4" = 1 | 0 1 2 3 4 5 6 7 8 9 10 11 12

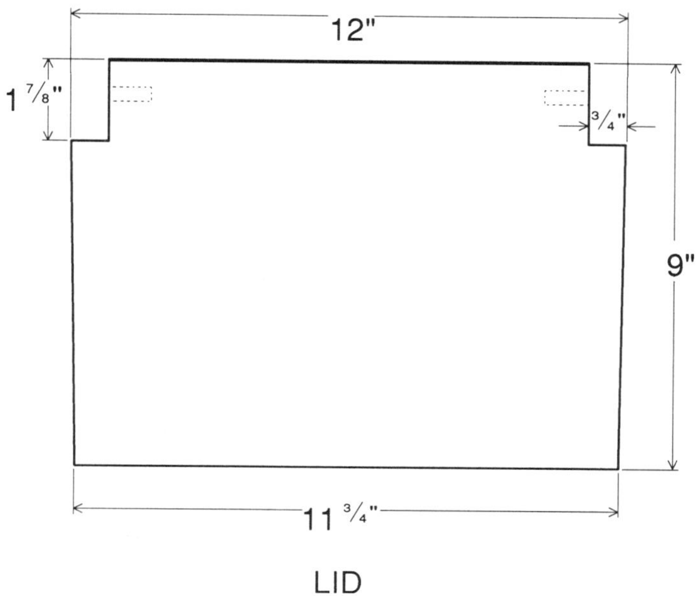

LID

INSTRUCTIONS

Medium level of difficulty

Use pine to make this box. Plane the sides down to a thickness of ¾", and fasten them with dovetail joints (see Introduction). Plane the bottom of the box and the lid to a thickness of ½". The bottom is fastened to the sides with wooden pegs. The lid sits with rounded tenons carved out of the lid material.

This box does not require finishing.

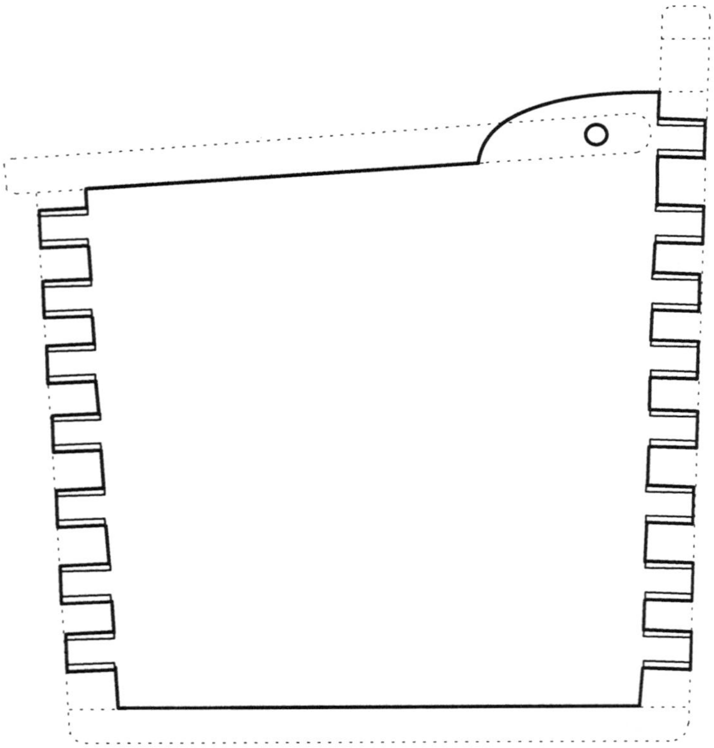

SIDE VIEW SHOWING DOVETAIL JOINTS

STOOL

This type of stool has been quite common since the 18th century. It has a rectangular seat with a hole for a handle, contoured legs and two short ends, as well as two long sides, which also serve to strengthen the seat.

Stools like this were commonly found in almost every home during the 18th and 19th centuries. They came in various sizes for various uses in the kitchen, parlor, and children's bedroom. Since the simple design requires a minimum of tools, these stools were convenient home handicraft products.

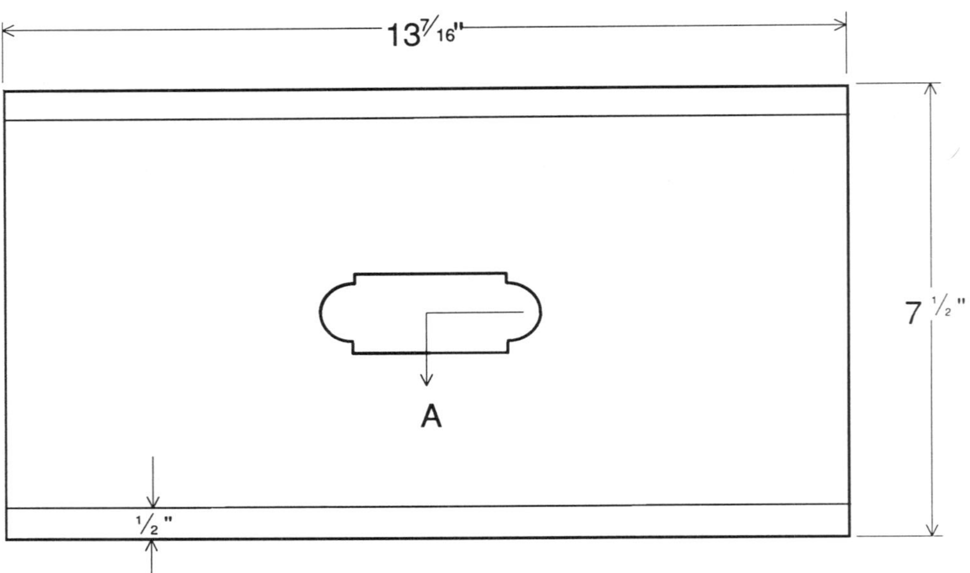

TOP VIEW

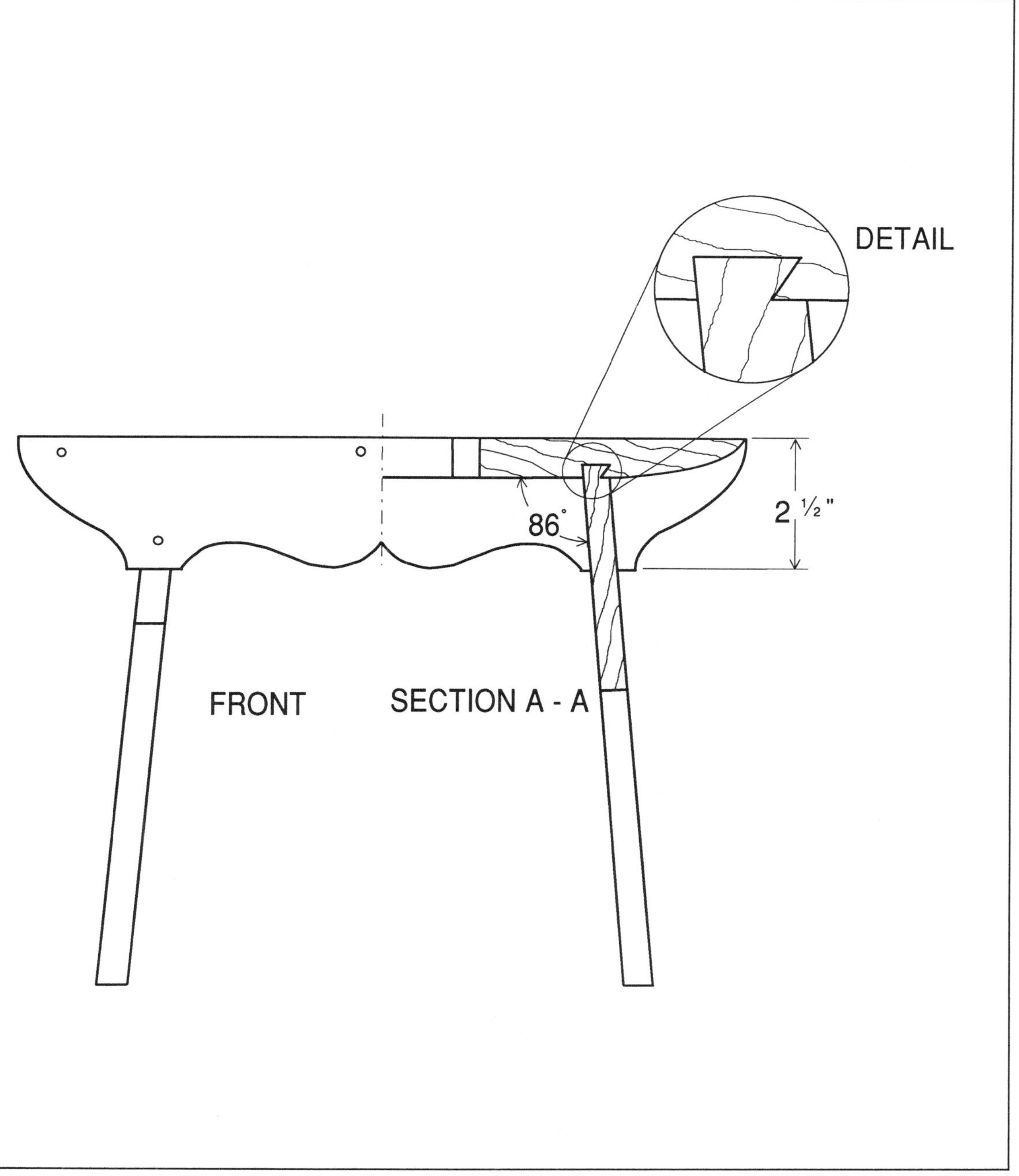
DETAIL
86°
2 ½"
FRONT
SECTION A - A

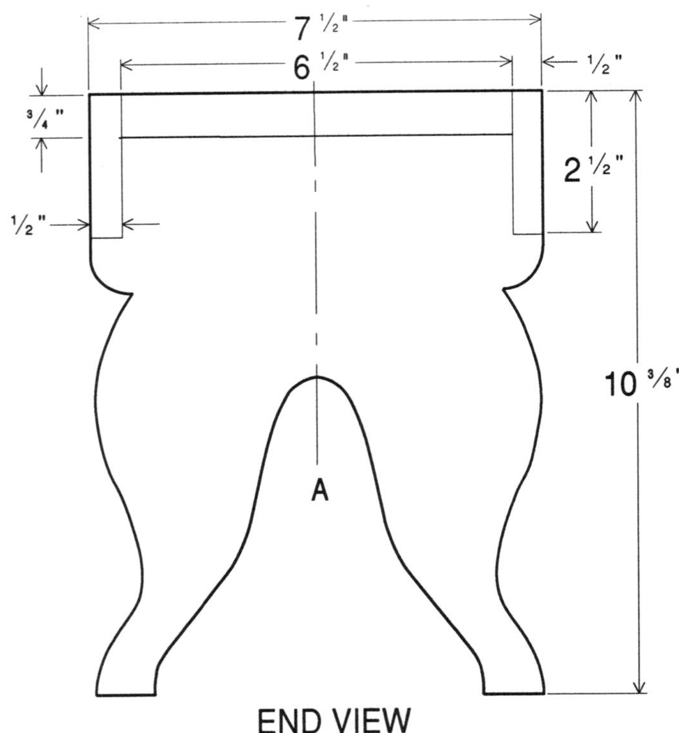

INSTRUCTIONS

Relatively easy to make

Use pine to make this stool. Plane the sides of the legs to a ¾" thickness, the seat to ¾", and the contoured edge pieces to ½". Fasten the sides of the legs to the seat with an angled bare-faced dovetail joint (see Introduction, joint #3). Fasten the edge pieces with wooden pegs into the seat and sides of the legs.

Paint the stool with reddish-brown linseed oil paint (burnt sienna).

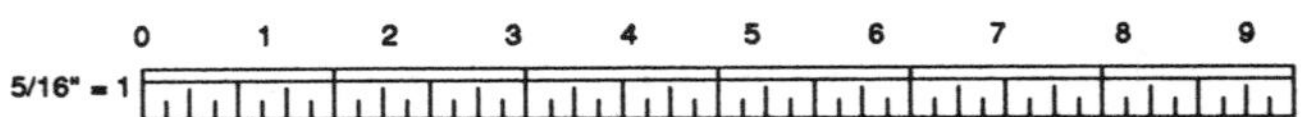

HIGH STOOL

Though this stool from eastern Bothnia in Finland (once part of Sweden) is not yet 100 years old, it preserves the ancient features which characterize the longstanding handicraft and furniture traditions of the region. The stool is quite worn and its light-gray color is only partially preserved.

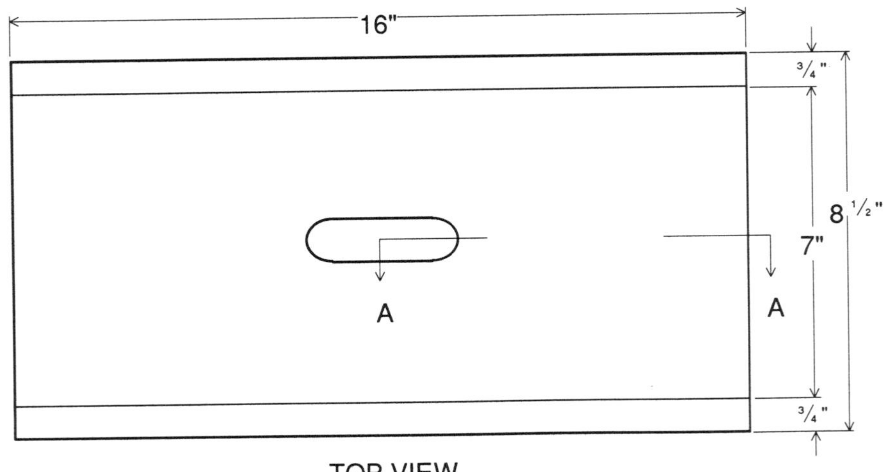

TOP VIEW

INSTRUCTIONS

Relatively easy to make

Use pine to make this stool. Plane the leg sides and the seat to a 3/4″ thickness. Plane the edge pieces to 3/4″, contour them, and fasten them to the seat with an angled bare-faced dovetail (see Introduction, joint #3). Use wooden pegs to fasten the edge pieces to both the seat and the legs' sides. Plane the cross rails to 1/2″ × 1 1/4″, set them into the legs, and fasten them with wooden pegs.

Paint the stool with gray linseed oil paint (a mixture of zinc white and burnt green earth).

1/4" = 1 0 1 2 3 4 5 6 7 8 9 10 11 12

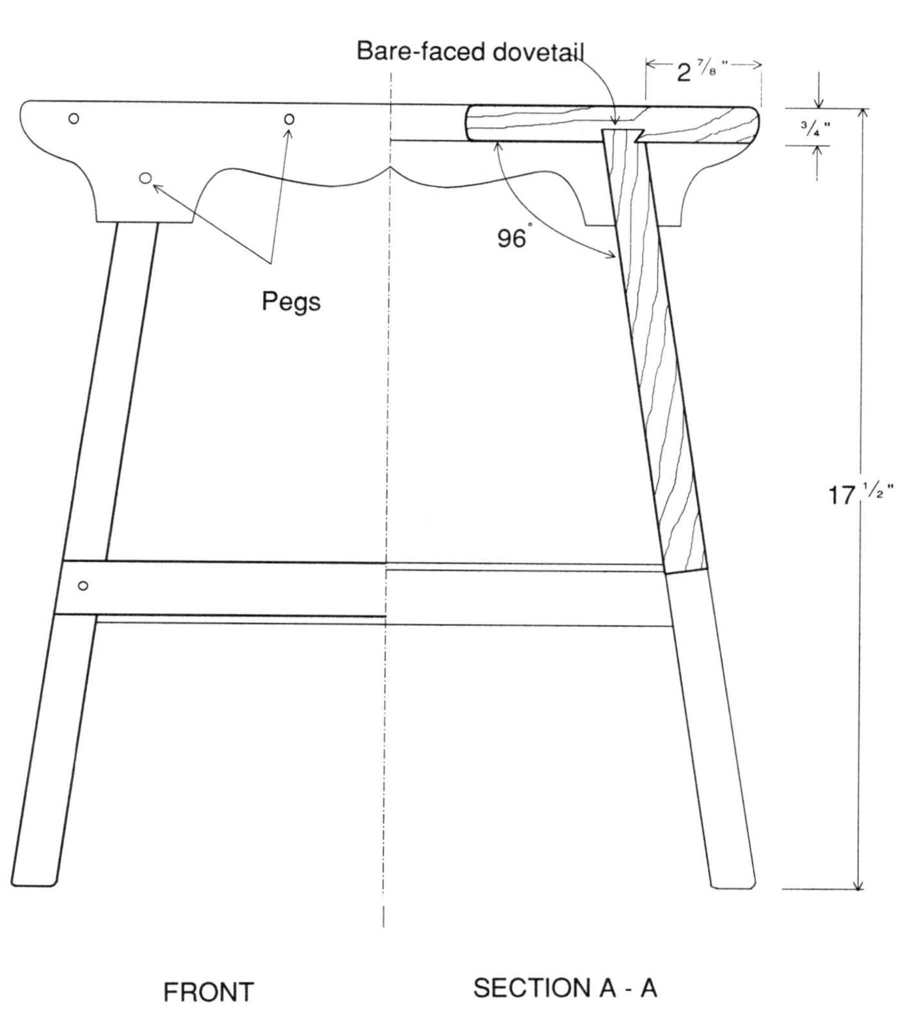
Bare-faced dovetail
2 7/8"
3/4"
96°
Pegs
17 1/2"
FRONT
SECTION A - A

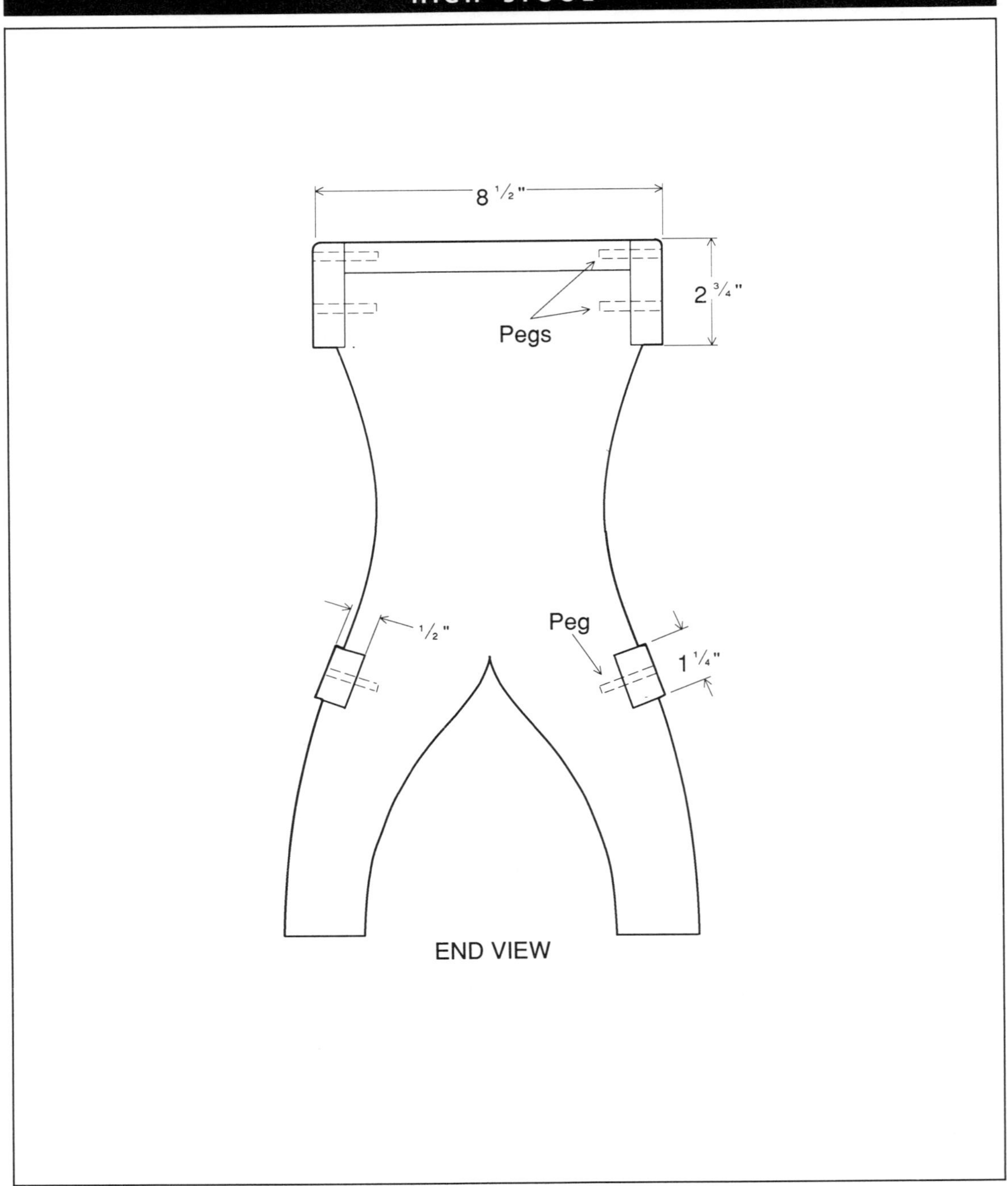
8 1/2"
2 3/4"
Pegs
1/2"
Peg
1 1/4"
END VIEW
0 1 2 3 4 5 6 7 8 9 10 11 12
1/4" = 1

CHILDREN'S STOOL

This small children's stool follows the same design as the other stools. It was made of pine, probably during the first half of the 18th century. Like many pieces of furniture from this period, it was originally painted pearl-gray, and then later a reddish-brown. At the beginning of the 19th century it was painted over with white paint and red borders. The many re-paintings partially conceal the profiles of the long sides and the oblique chamfers of the legs.

The three stacked stools in the photograph on page 50 are from the parlor of the Näs manor house in Rö, a province of Uppland. They are made of pine and painted white.

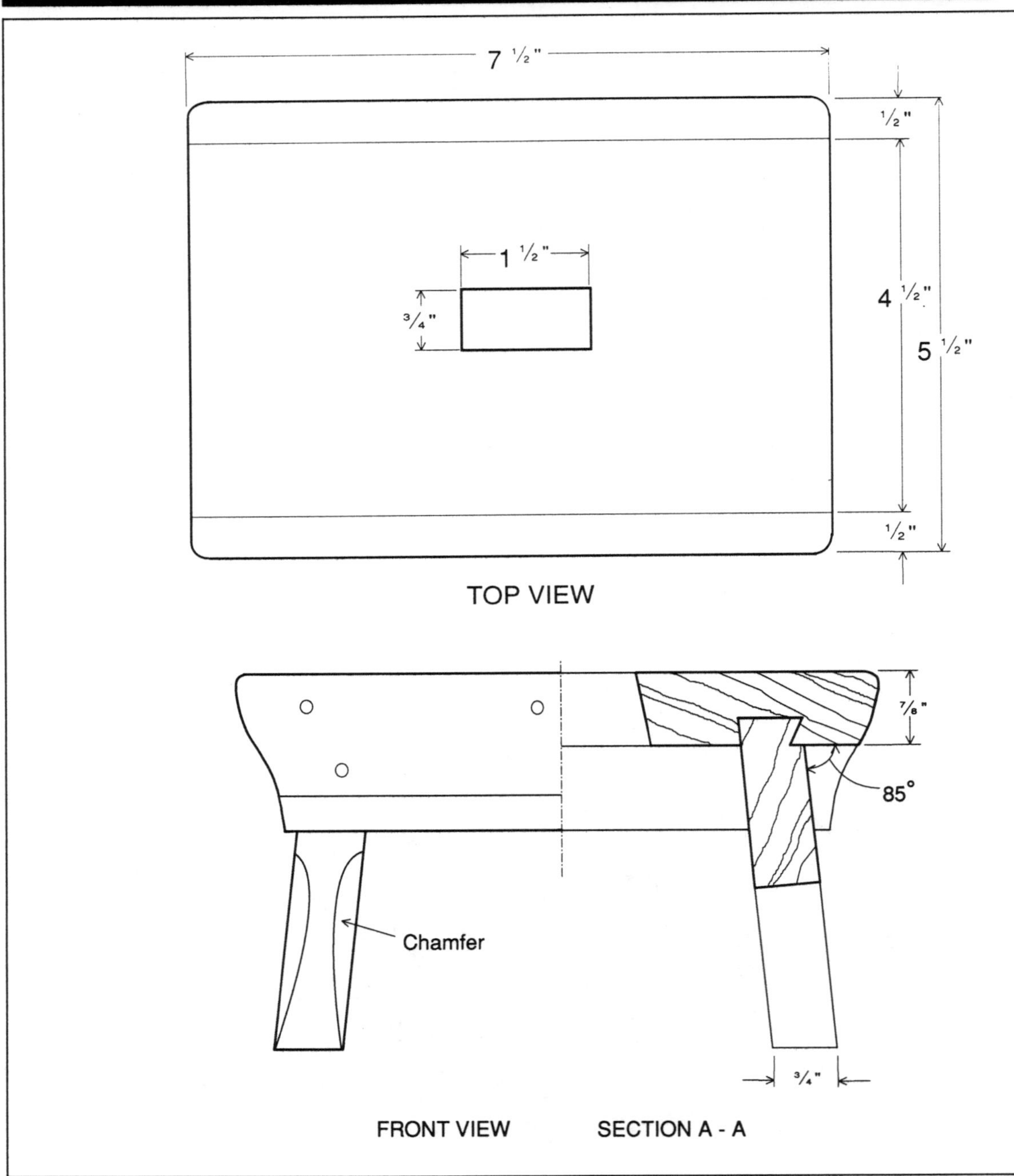
7 1/2"
1/2"
1 1/2"
3/4"
4 1/2"
5 1/2"
1/2"
TOP VIEW
7/8"
85°
Chamfer
3/4"
FRONT VIEW
SECTION A - A

1/2" = 1
0 1 2 3 4 5 6

INSTRUCTIONS

Relatively easy to make

Use pine to make this stool. Plane the sides of the legs to a ¾″ thickness, and the seat to ⅞″. Plane the edge pieces down to ½″, and profile them with a molding plane, router, or shaper, on the lower edge. Fasten the leg sides to the seat with an angled bare-faced dovetail (see Introduction, joint #3). Fasten the edge pieces to both the seat and the sides of the legs with wooden pegs.

Paint the stool with linseed oil paint in a reddish-brown color (burnt sienna), or in pearl-gray (zinc white mixed with burnt green earth).

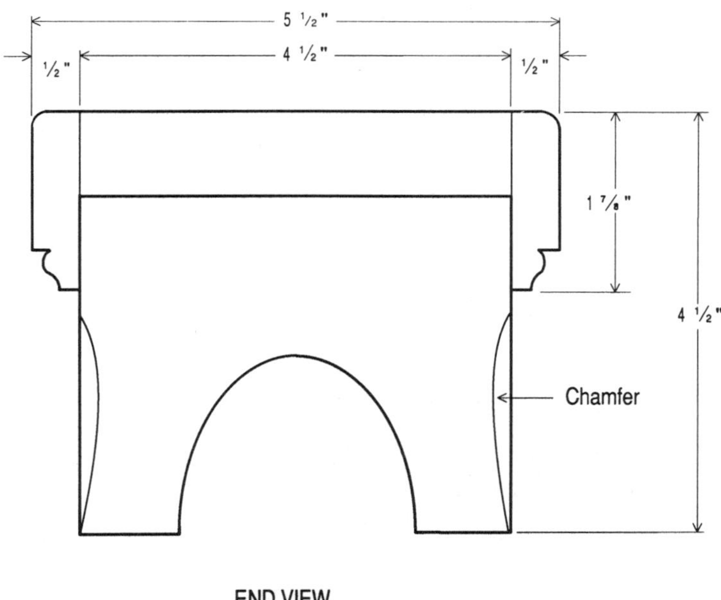

END VIEW

CHILDREN'S STOOL

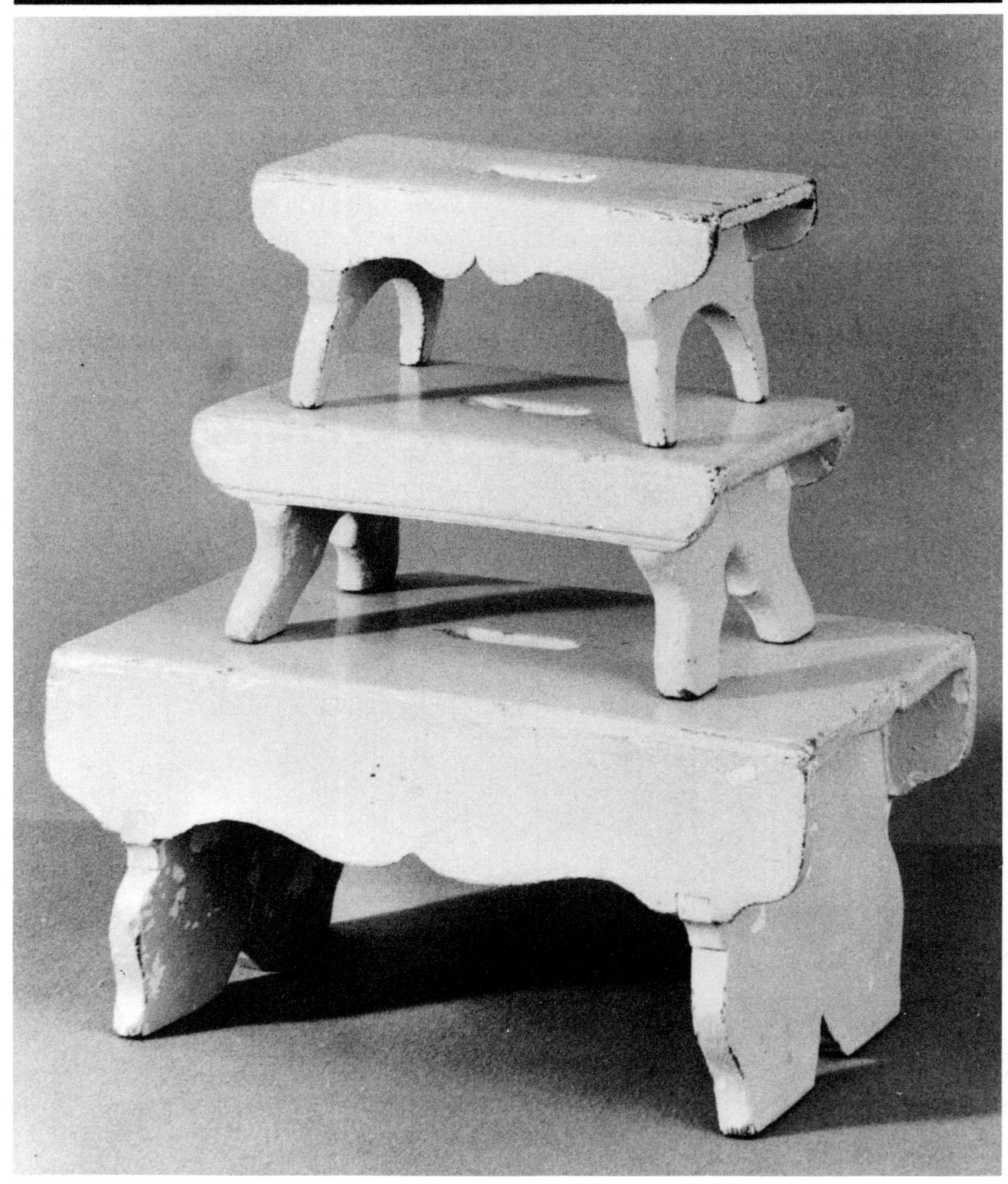

PLANK LADDER

This plank ladder is in a manor house in Ostgötland on the island of Götland, probably from the latter half of the 18th century. The original design consists quite simply of a selected straight plank with sawed-out holes as rungs. But even this very simple unpainted attic and pantry ladder exhibits carefully shaped details: the edges are molded, the foot end is contoured, and the "rungs" are identical and precisely sawed out.

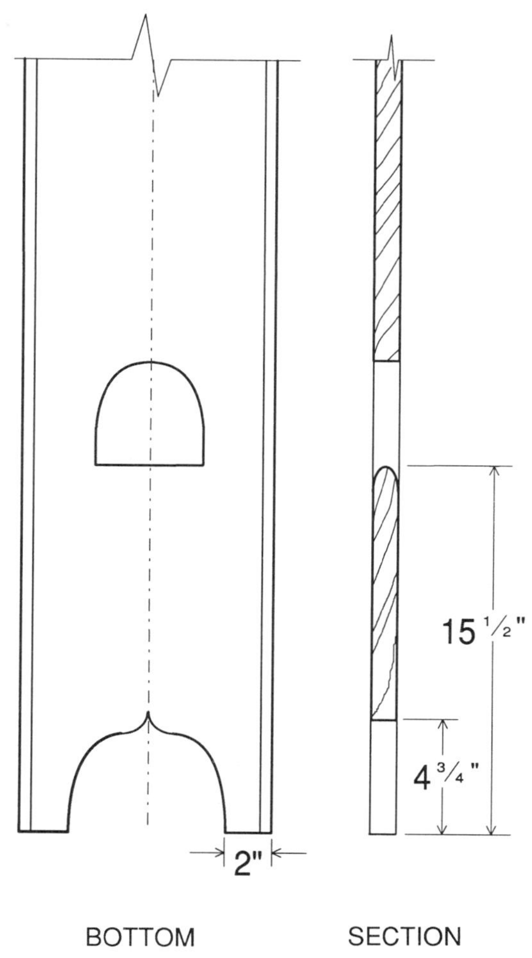

1/8" = 1 — 0 2 4 6 8 10 12 14 16 18 20 22 24

PLANK LADDER

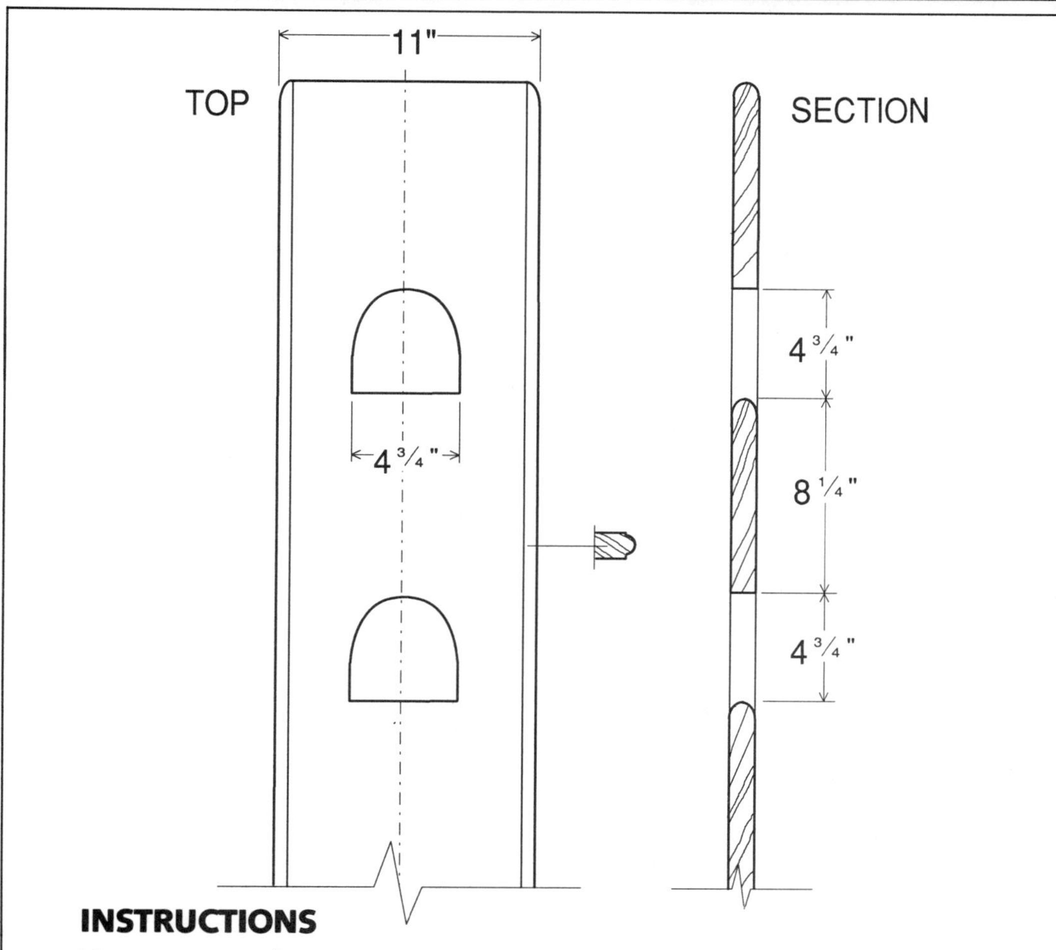

INSTRUCTIONS

Very easy to make

Use a pine plank to make this ladder. Plane it down to 1″ thick. Then plane the outer edges with a molding plane, router, or shaper. Adjust the length of the ladder to suit your requirements. The original model is 8′ long, and 1′ wide. Saw out the cutouts for the footholds with a compass saw. Round the edges, especially the edge on which you set your foot.

This ladder can be brushed with a mixture of linseed oil and turpentine.

1/8" = 1 0 2 4 6 8 10 12 14 16 18 20 22 24

STEPLADDER

This small fold-up stepladder is in the guest-room wing of the Skogaholm manor house at the Skansen exhibit, and is painted grayish-green with linseed oil paint. It was probably made during the second half of the 18th century. The playfully wavy profiles can best be described as a sort of country rococo. The ladder and the support are connected at the top by an iron rod, which functions as a hinge.

Fold-up ladders came into daily use in Sweden during the age of wax and paraffin candles, when ceiling and wall lights had to be lit, trimmed, and snuffed. They were usually painted with oil paint.

The smaller stepladder (see photo, page 59) is in the storeroom of the Skogaholm manor house, at the Skansen exhibit. This simpler type of stepladder was being made into the 19th century.

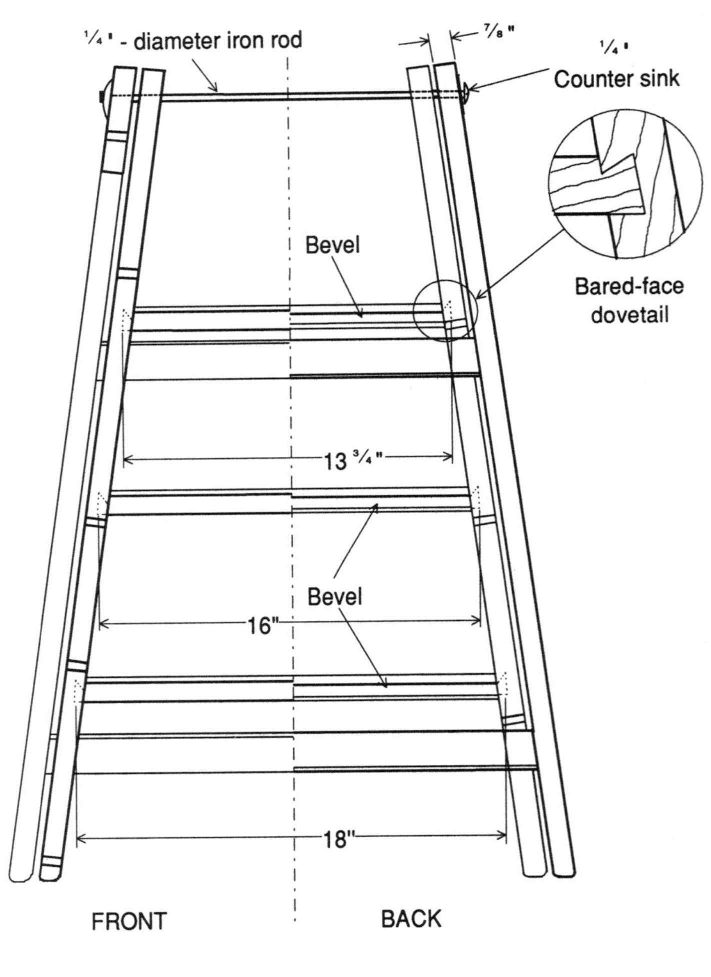

0 2 4 6 8 10 12 14 16 18 20 22 24

1/8" = 1

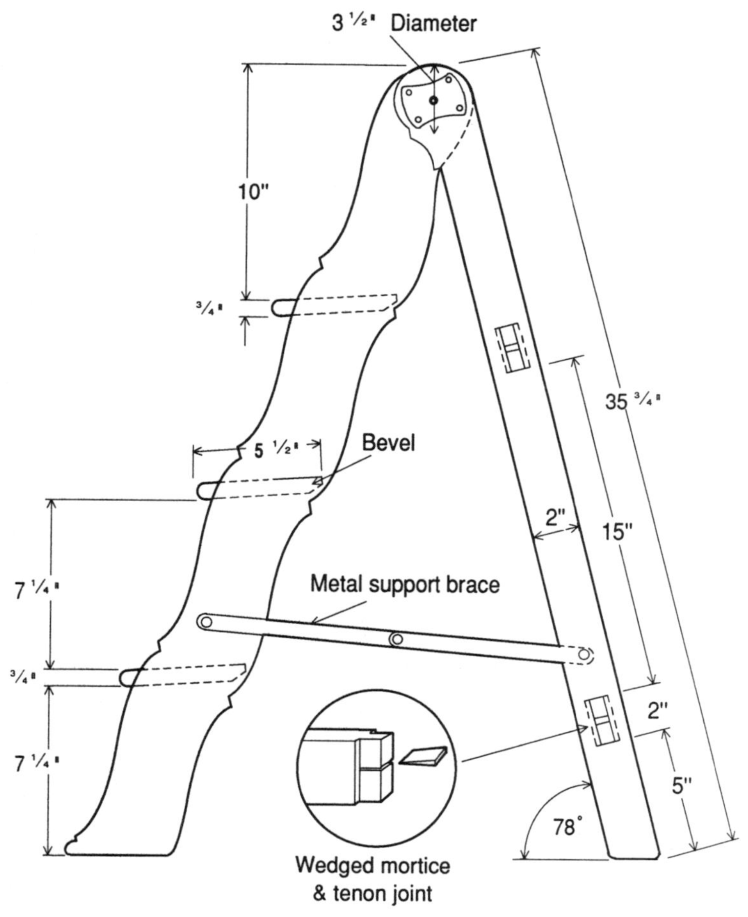
3 1/2" Diameter
10"
3/4"
5 1/2"
Bevel
7 1/4"
3/4"
7 1/4"
Metal support brace
35 3/4"
2"
15"
2"
5"
78°
Wedged mortice
& tenon joint

INSTRUCTIONS

Fairly difficult to make

Use pine to make this ladder. Plane the side pieces to a thickness of 7⁄8″. Contour them, and attach them to the flat treads which should be planed to a thickness of 3⁄4″. Attach them using a stopped, bare-faced dovetail (see Introduction, joint #2). The mortise ends approximately 1″ inside the trailing edge of the flat sides.

Plane the supporting legs to 7⁄8″ thick. Cut the round end at the top to a diameter of 3½″, and make the support legs 2″ wide. Plane the two crossbars to ½″ × 2″. Shape the short ends into 3⁄8″ thick tenons. Insert the tenons through the support legs and wedge them in place.

Attach the support legs to the ladder with a ¼″ diameter iron rod. One end of the rod should have a hemispherical head with a groove for a screwdriver, and the other end should be threaded. A forged fitting with a threaded hole is fastened with a nail or screw to the outside of the support leg. Or a countersunk washer and nut could be used instead.

If none are available commercially, make two hinged support leg braces from flat steel bars, 1⁄8″ × 5⁄8″. Alternatively, the support leg can be locked in place by means of a strong rope. The support leg braces which are now on the original model are probably not the original ones. They should have been longer so that the flat steps did not tilt forward. So make your support leg braces somewhat longer or move them higher up on the ladder. If you wish, you can use readily available lid support braces as leg braces.

Paint the ladder with gray linseed oil paint, a mixture of zinc white and burnt green earth.

RECTANGULAR LANTERN

While this hand lantern or stable lantern of unpainted pine comes from Lagga in Uppland province, its type was in common everyday use in many parts of the country. The cover and bottom are two square pieces of wood connected by four corner posts with sawed-out tracks for the glass, which does not need to be puttied or nailed. By raising the two-part glass, the candle in the lantern becomes accessible. In the cover a smoke-hole was sawed out and covered by a curved metal plate. A candle holder of sheet metal was fastened on the bottom.

INSTRUCTIONS

Easy to make

Use pine to make this lantern. Bore holes in the bottom and top plates for the tenons of the posts. Make another hole in the top plate for ventilation, and fasten a wire handle with nails from the underside. Above the ventilation hole fasten a curved metal plate with nails. Saw or chisel grooves in the posts for the glass panes. Secure the tenons of the posts with nails or wooden pegs. Have the tenons stick up on the top side above the cover plate, secured with nails or wooden pegs. The glass panes should sit loosely in the grooves. Gouge a notch in the bottom for a fingerhold to raise the sliding glass panel. Three pieces of glass, $4\frac{13}{16} \times 10\frac{15}{16}$ and two pieces, $14\frac{13}{16} \times 6''$, will be needed.

Brush the lantern with a mixture of linseed oil and turpentine.

Note: For fire safety reasons, use a candleholder made of metal.

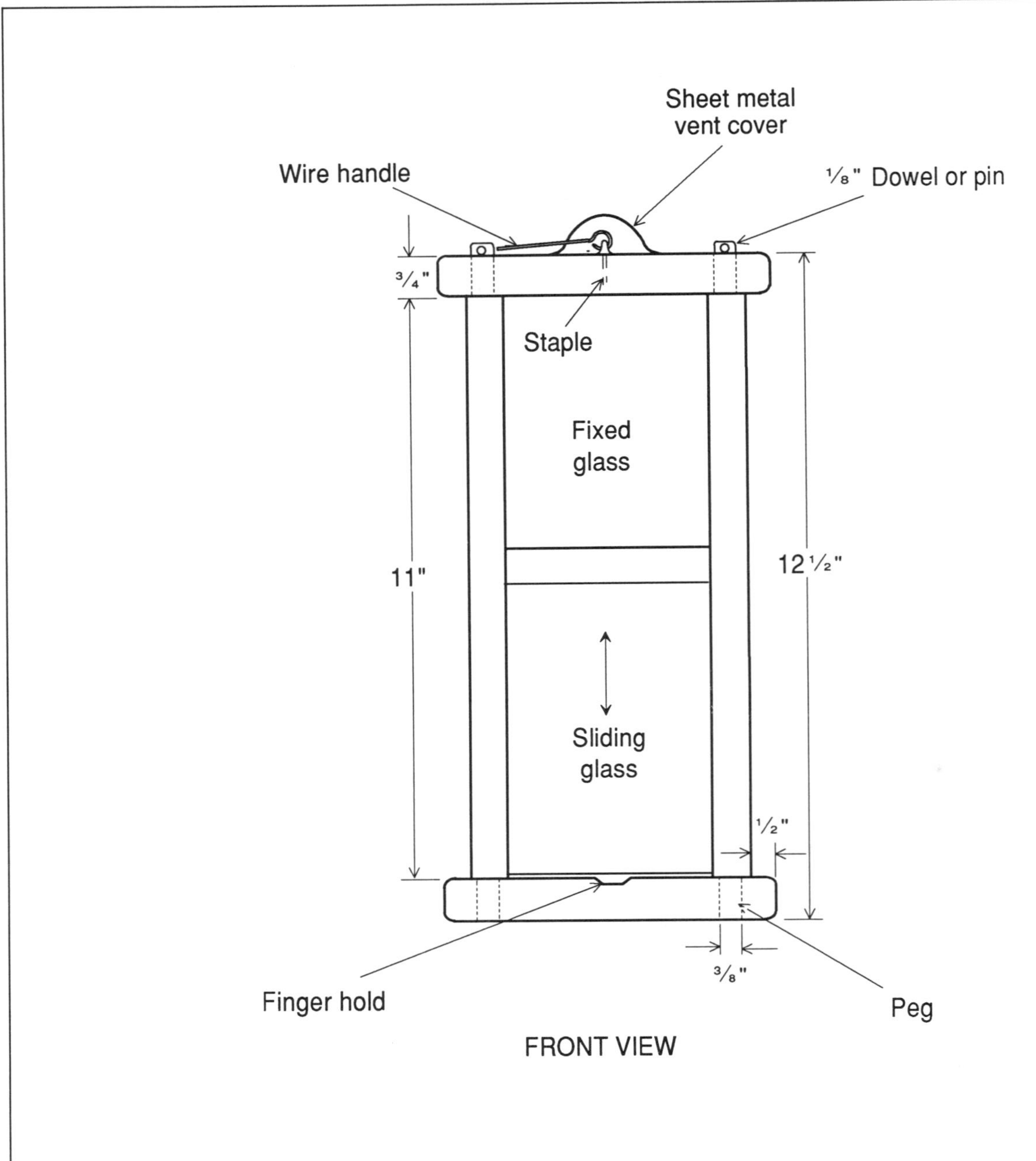
Sheet metal
vent cover
Wire handle
1/8" Dowel or pin
3/4"
Staple
Fixed
glass
11"
12 1/2"
Sliding
glass
1/2"
3/8"
Finger hold
Peg
FRONT VIEW
0 1 2 3 4 5 6 7 8 9
5/16" = 1

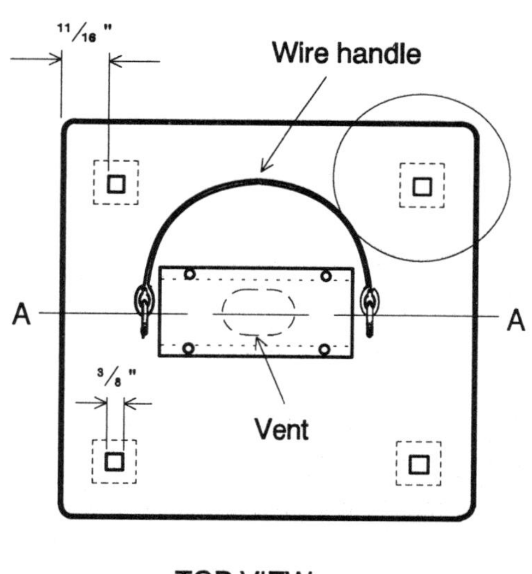

TOP VIEW

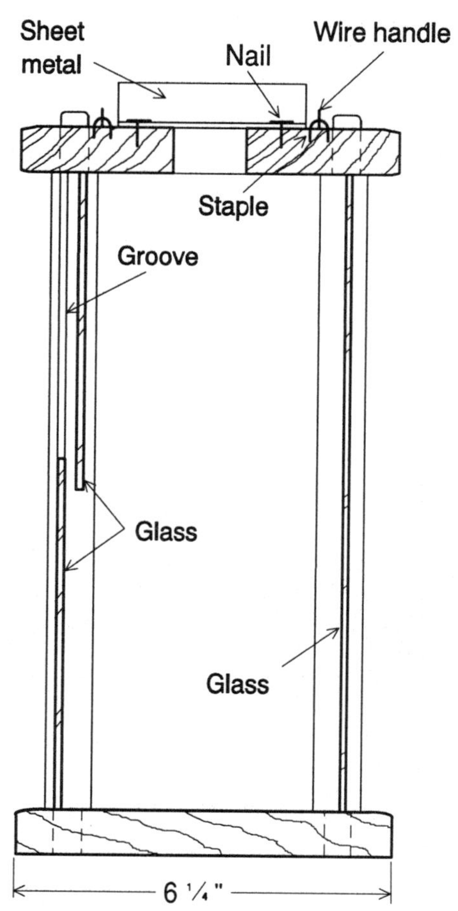

SECTION A-A

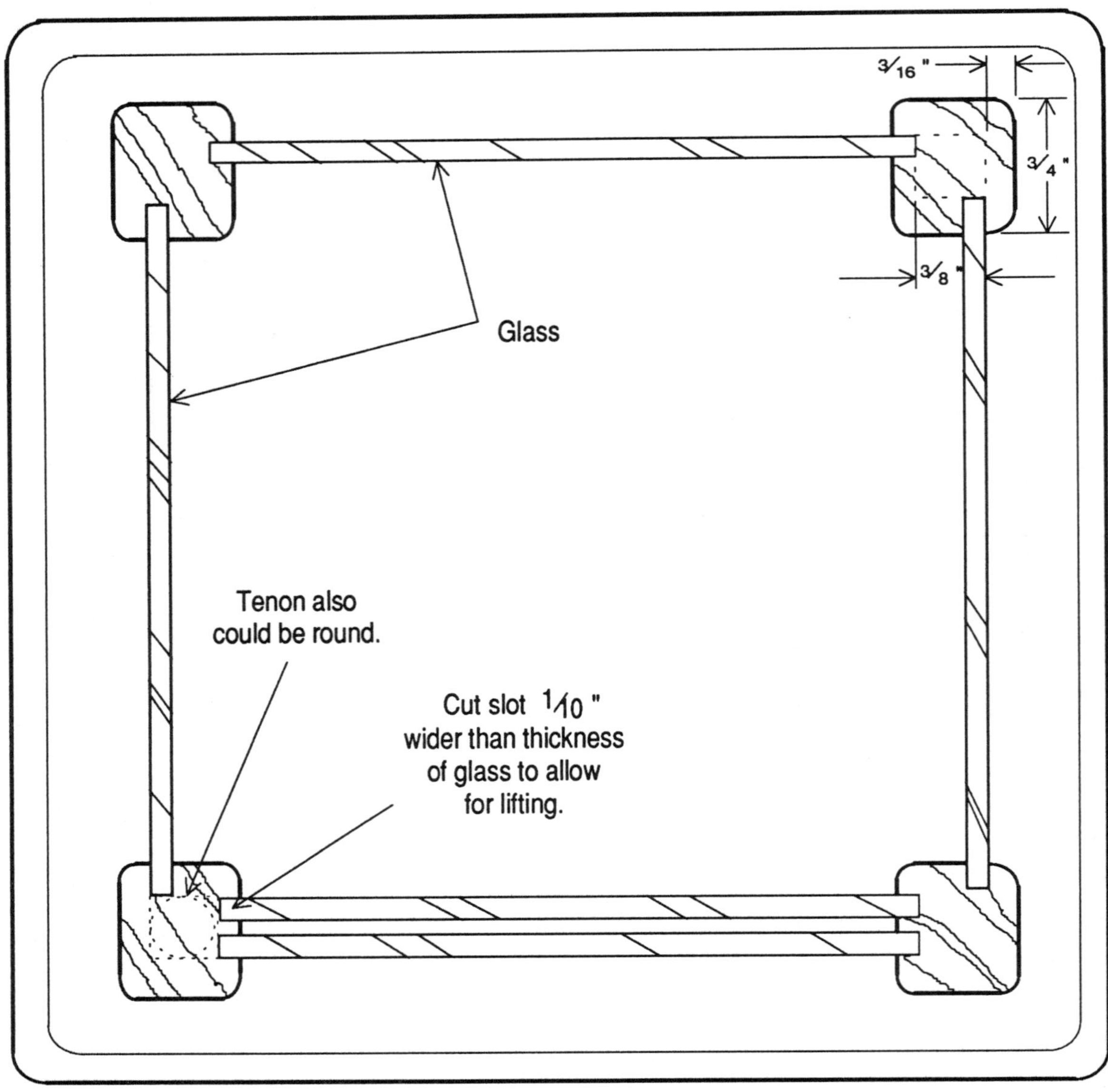
3⁄16"
3⁄4"
3⁄8"
Glass
Tenon also could be round.
Cut slot 1⁄10" wider than thickness of glass to allow for lifting.

ACTUAL SIZE DETAIL

TOP VIEW SECTION

OCTAGONAL LANTERN

This octagonal lantern is from the province of Uppland, and was made at the end of the 18th century or the first half of the 19th century. It is a hand lantern of unpainted pine, and could also be hung from the ceiling or on a nail in the wall—a somewhat more developed variant of the usual four-cornered stable lantern.

The bottom and top are octagonal pieces of wood, connected by eight corner posts which surround the glass panes. A contoured hole was sawed out of the top for smoke and heat, and a carrying handle of thick steel wire was attached. The glass in the door is surrounded by four frame pieces. The door is fastened with pin hinges, but on other lanterns of this type, nailed leather pieces or ordinary small articulated hinges were used.

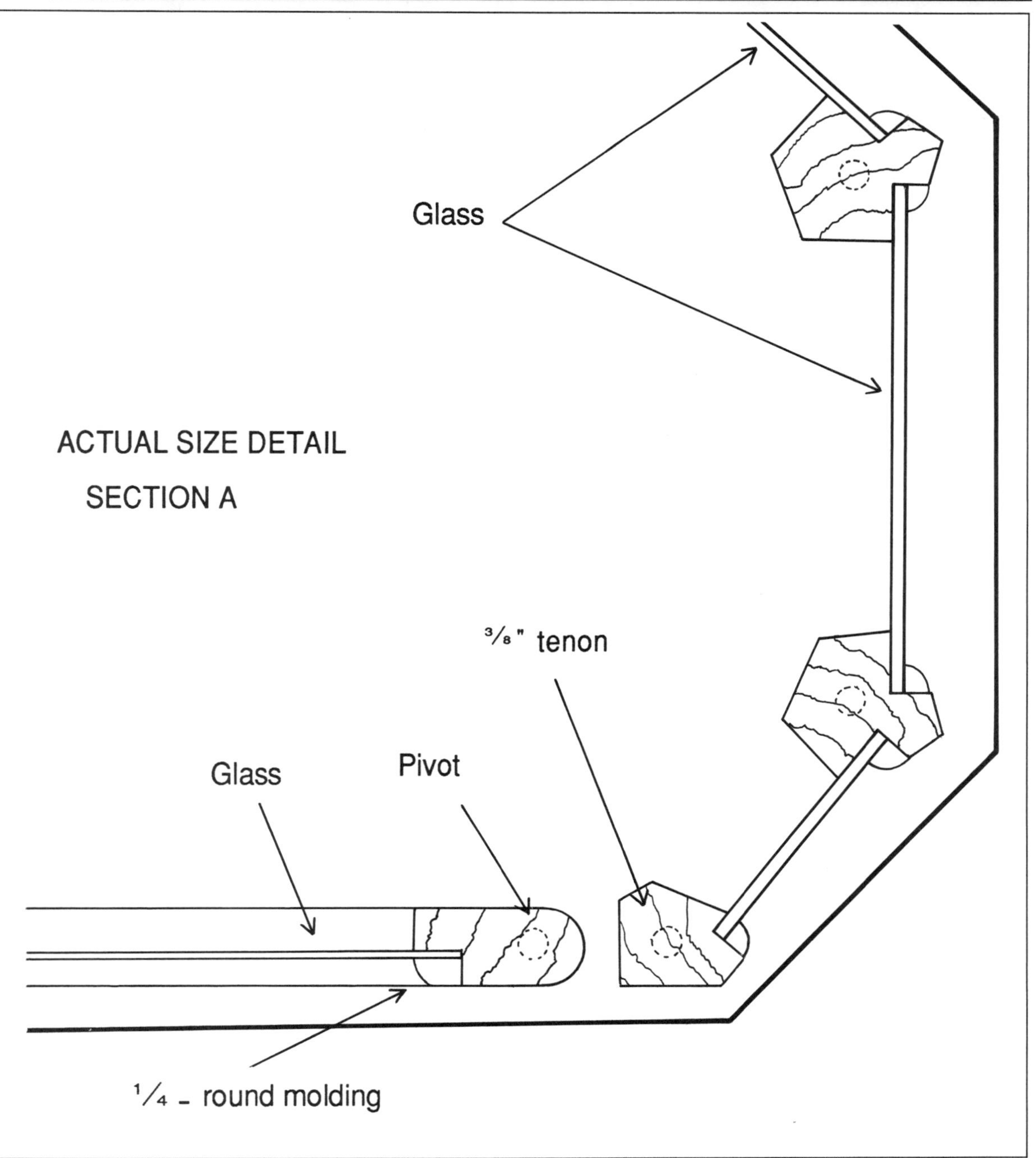
Glass
ACTUAL SIZE DETAIL
SECTION A
3/8" tenon
Glass
Pivot
1/4 - round molding

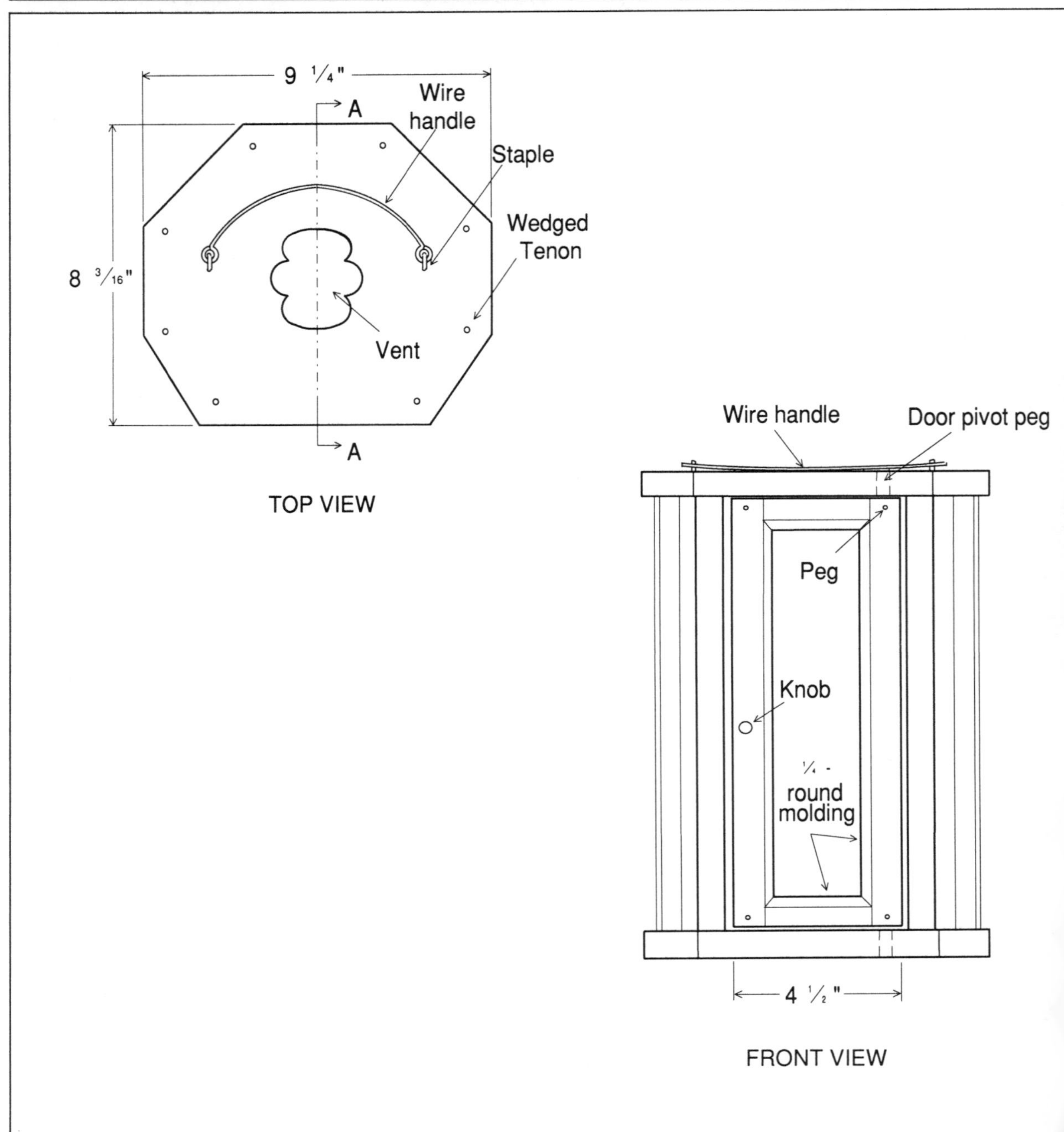
9 1/4"
A
Wire
handle
Staple
Wedged
Tenon
8 3/16"
Vent
A
TOP VIEW
Wire handle
Door pivot peg
Peg
Knob
1/4 -
round
molding
4 1/2"
FRONT VIEW
0 1 2 3 4 5 6 7 8 9 10 11 12
1/4" = 1

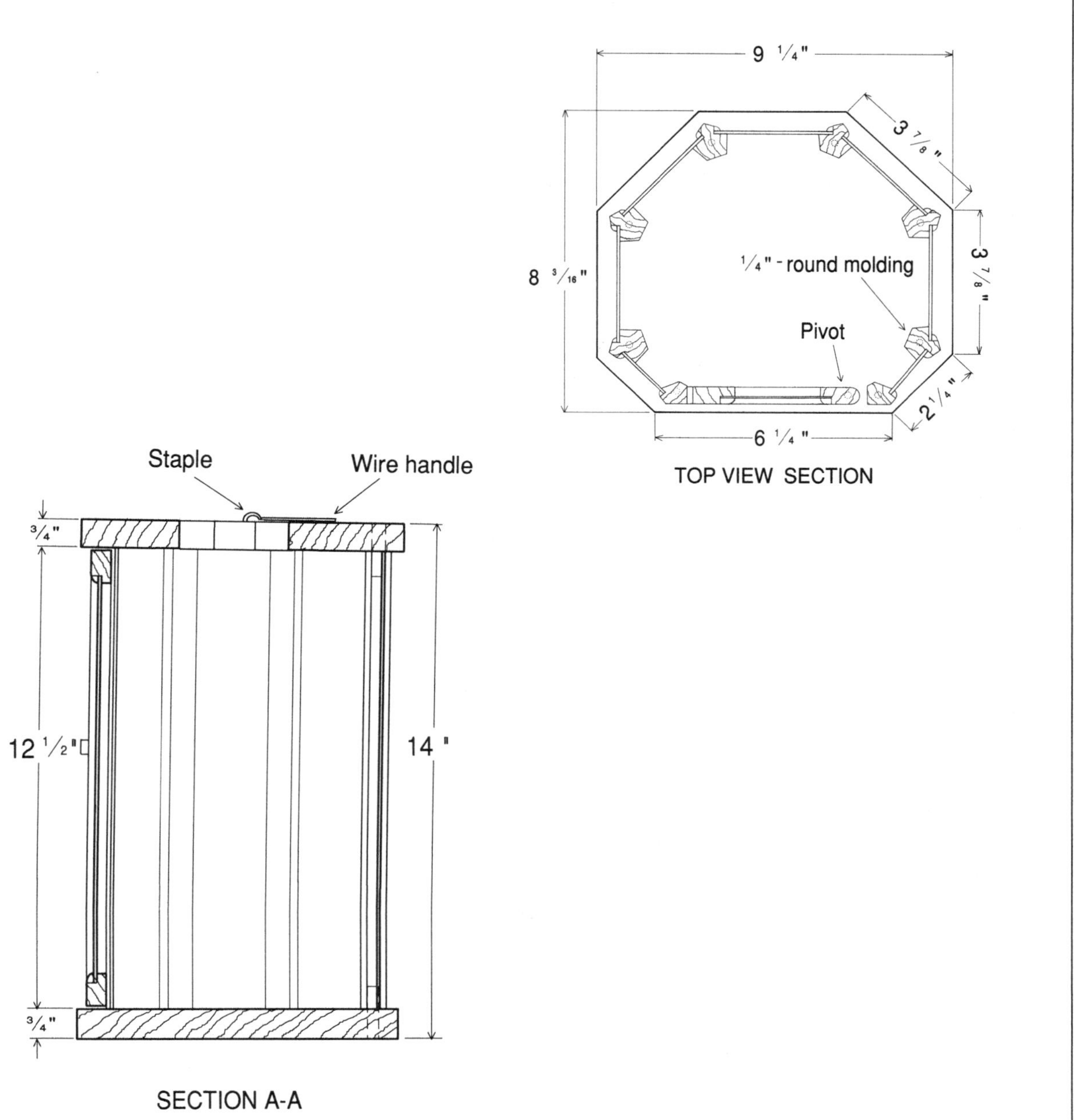

TOP VIEW SECTION

SECTION A-A

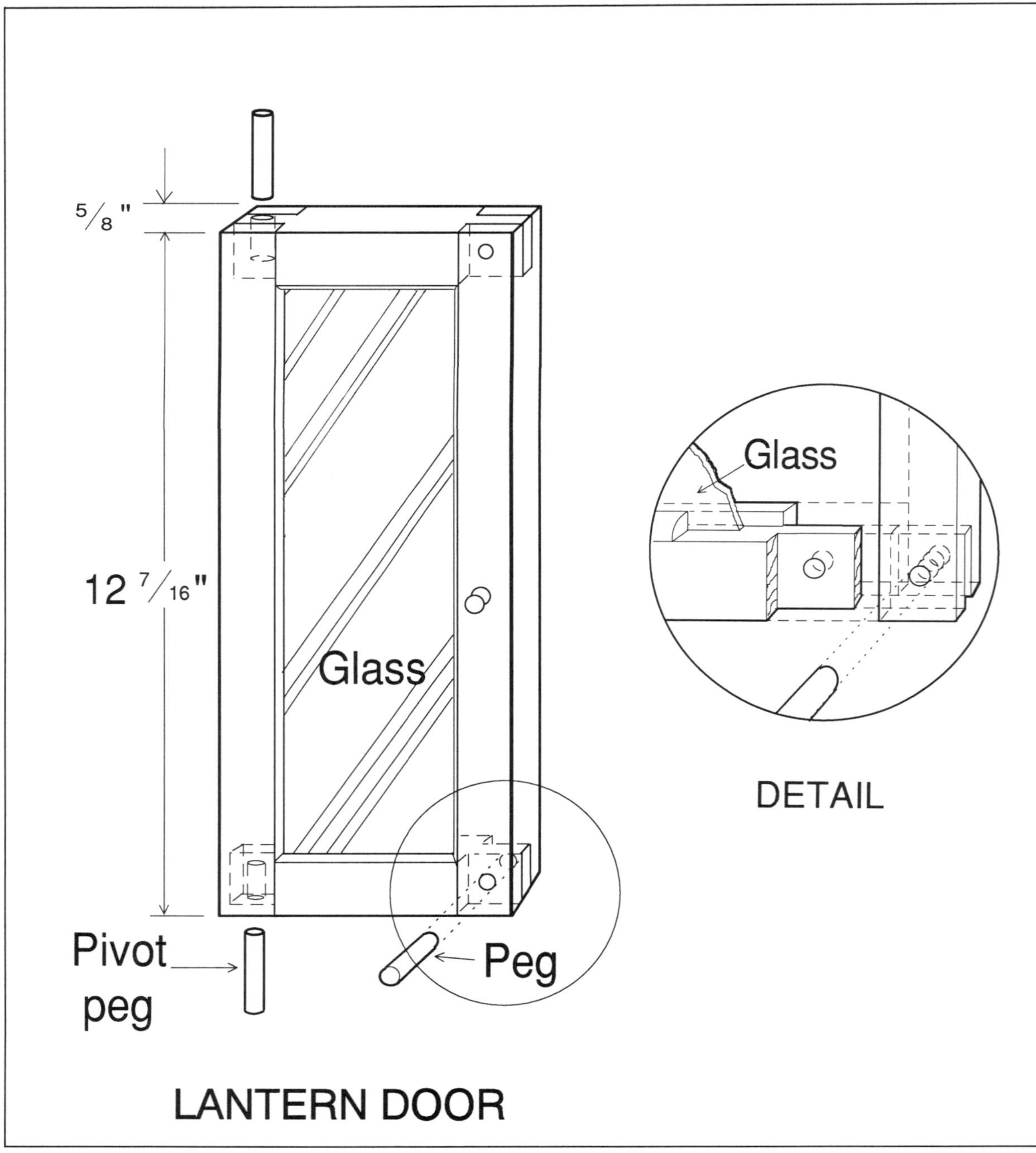
5/8"
12 7/16"
Glass
Pivot peg
Peg
Glass
DETAIL
LANTERN DOOR

0 1 2 3 4 5 6 7 8
3/8" = 1

INSTRUCTIONS

Difficult to make

Use pine to make this lantern. Drill holes in the bottom and top plates for the tenon-shaped ends of the posts. Cut a hole in the top plate for ventilation. Use eye-screws to attach a wire handle. Saw grooves for the glass into the eight posts.

Rabbet the framing members of the door to hold the glass. The glass is then held in place with ¼-round molding. Rabbet the corner posts, and secure them with round wooden wedged tenons. The door has butt hinges and a wooden pull-knob. After assembly wedge the wooden pegs that attach the posts. Then fasten the glass in place with brads and putty, or ¼-round molding. Measure and cut the glass after assembly..

The lantern can be brushed with a mixture of linseed oil and turpentine.

TOOL SHELF

This contour-sawed shelf is in Älvrosgården, at the Skansen exhibit. Where the shelf was used to store tools, kitchen knives, or the like, holes were made for them through the shelf. To support the shelf, a bracket should be put under it, so that the shelf does not break off.

The original model is shown in place on a wall. The newly made shelf is shown before holes were drilled in it for tools.

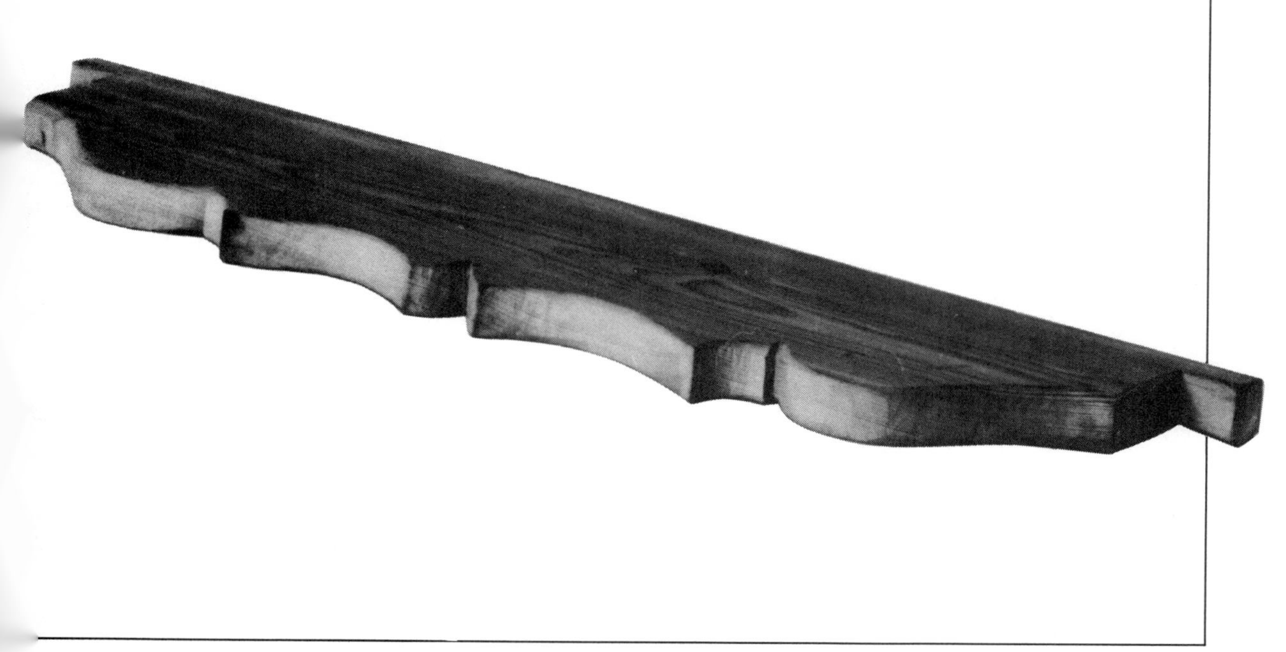

INSTRUCTIONS

Very easy to make

Use pine to make this shelf. Plane it to a 1″ thickness. Contour and bevel the edges. If you wish, fasten a bracket to the shelf with nails or wooden plugs. (Either of the shelf brackets which follow would give the needed support.) The bracket and shelf are fastened to the wall with hanging mounts or screws.

The original model is unfinished, but the shelf can be brushed with a mixture of linseed oil and turpentine.

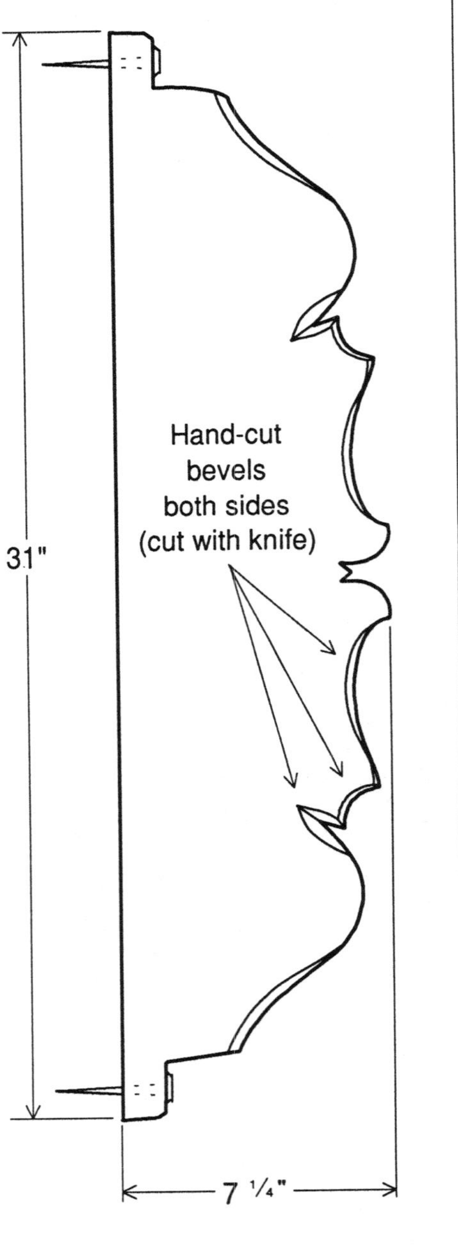

3/16" = 1
0 1 2 3 4 5 6 7 8 9 10 11 12 13 14 15 16

BRACKETS FOR SHELVES

These brackets for single shelves are both at the exhibit in Skansen. One is in a living room in Älvrosgården, and the other is in the kitchen of Skogaholm's manor house. In the photograph on page 78, the tool shelf described previously and the towel holder described on page 97 can also be seen on the wall below the shelf.

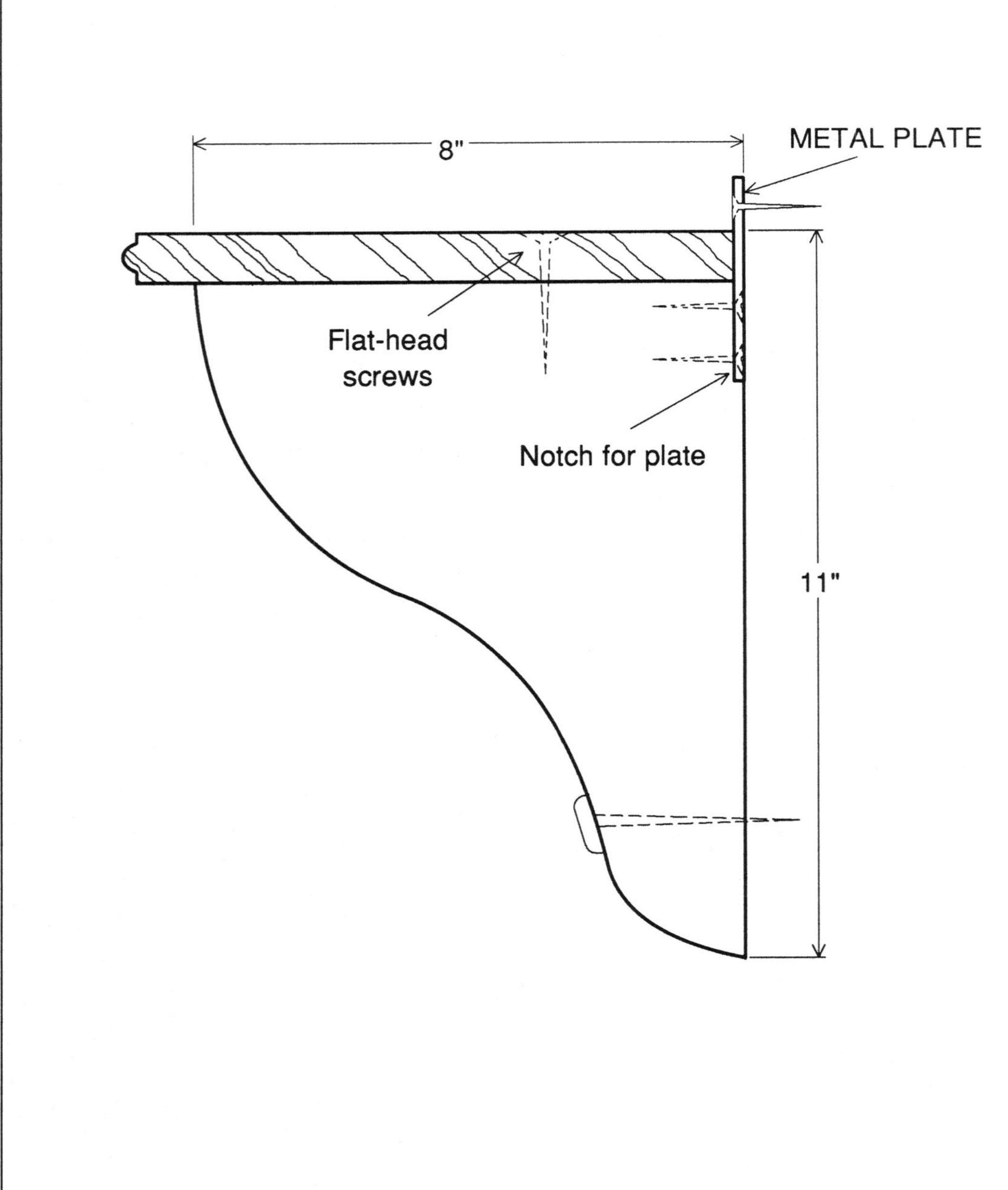
8"
METAL PLATE
Flat-head
screws
Notch for plate
11"
0 1 2 3 4 5 6 7 8
3/8" = 1

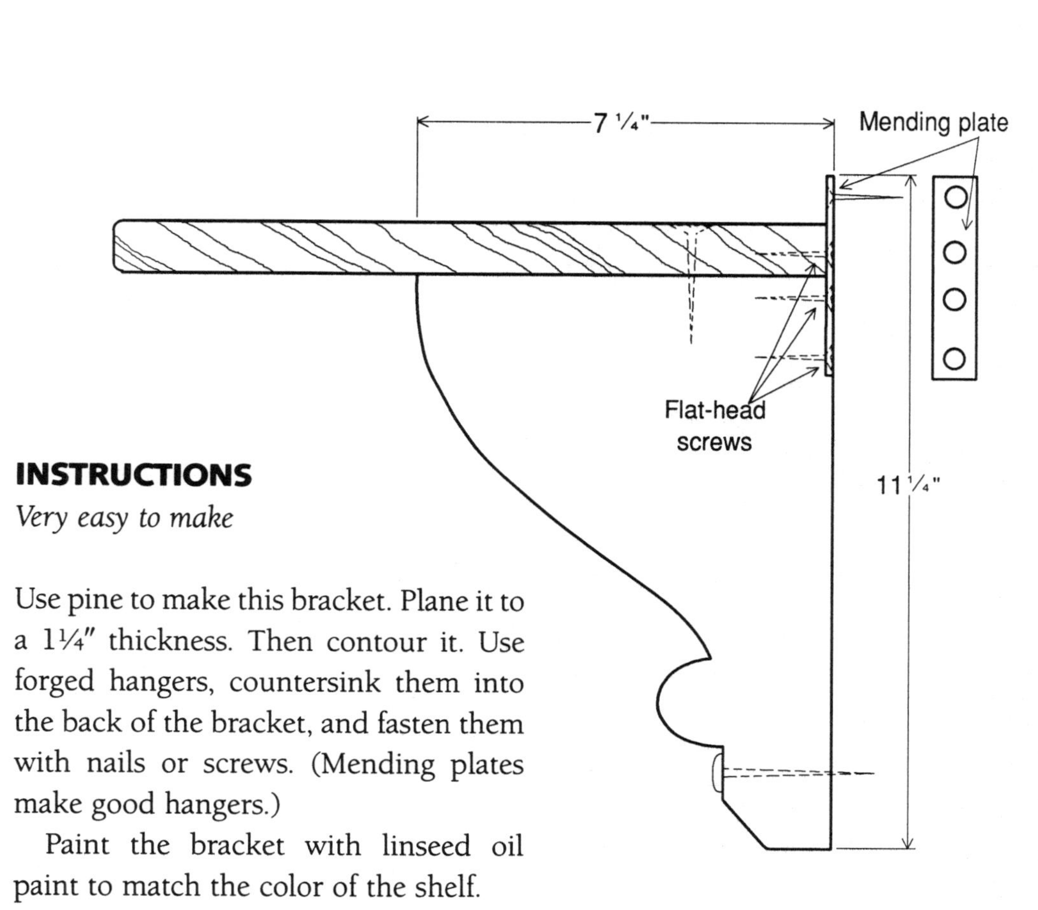

INSTRUCTIONS

Very easy to make

Use pine to make this bracket. Plane it to a 1¼" thickness. Then contour it. Use forged hangers, countersink them into the back of the bracket, and fasten them with nails or screws. (Mending plates make good hangers.)

Paint the bracket with linseed oil paint to match the color of the shelf.

5/16" = 1 0 1 2 3 4 5 6 7 8 9

PEG BOARDS

Here are three variations of simple peg boards that in the past were ordinarily used for hanging up clothes. They are still to be found, often several feet long, in cloakrooms and in the attics of old houses. The most common and perhaps oldest type is the one with carved pegs or hooks, often completely unpainted. During the 19th century, painted coat racks with turned pegs became more common.

A less common type of clothes rack is the one consisting of contoured semicircular boards on projecting supports. (See photo, page 82.)

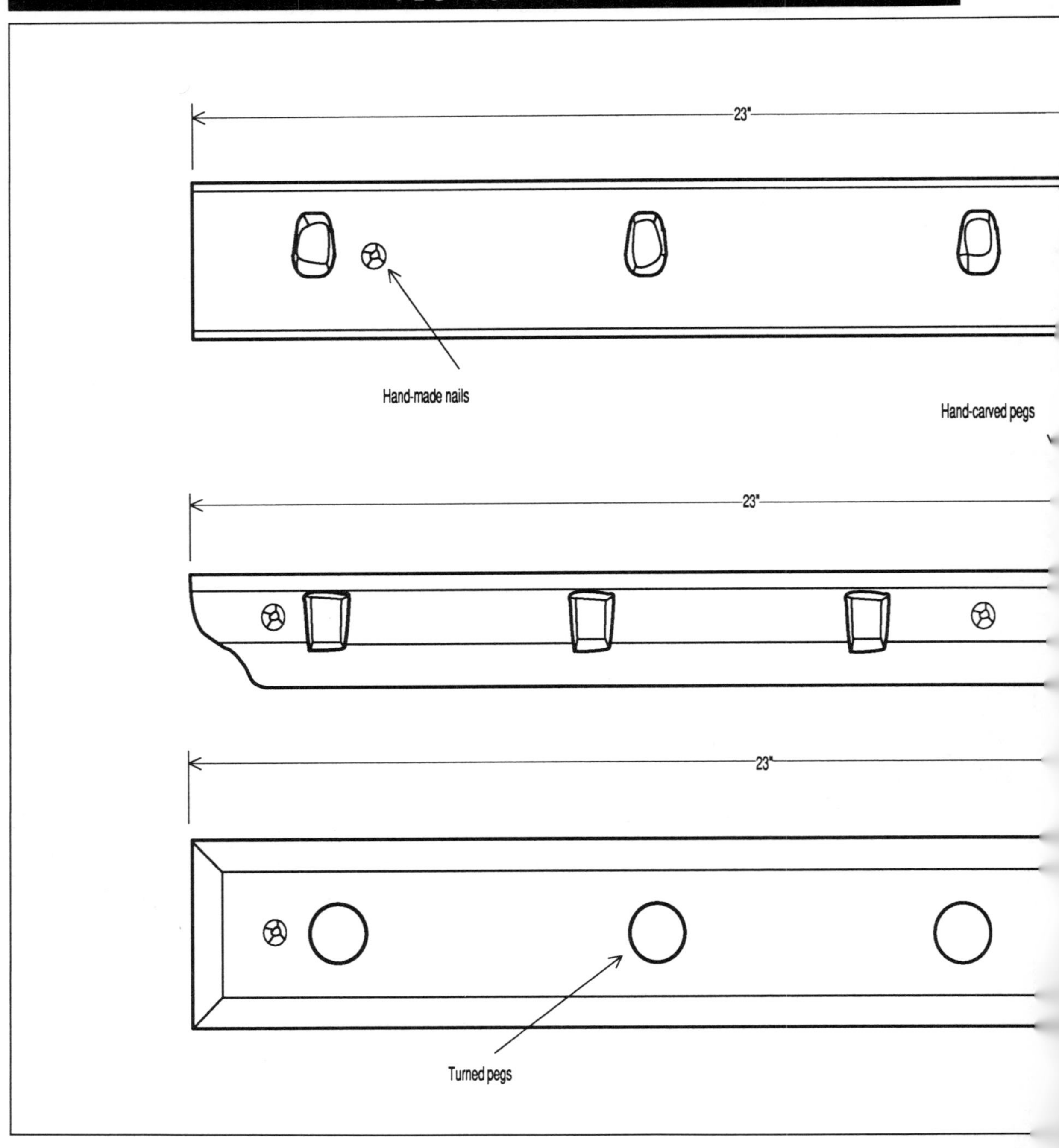
23"
Hand-made nails
Hand-carved pegs
23"
23"
Turned pegs
0 1 2 3 4 5 6 7 8 9
5/16" = 1

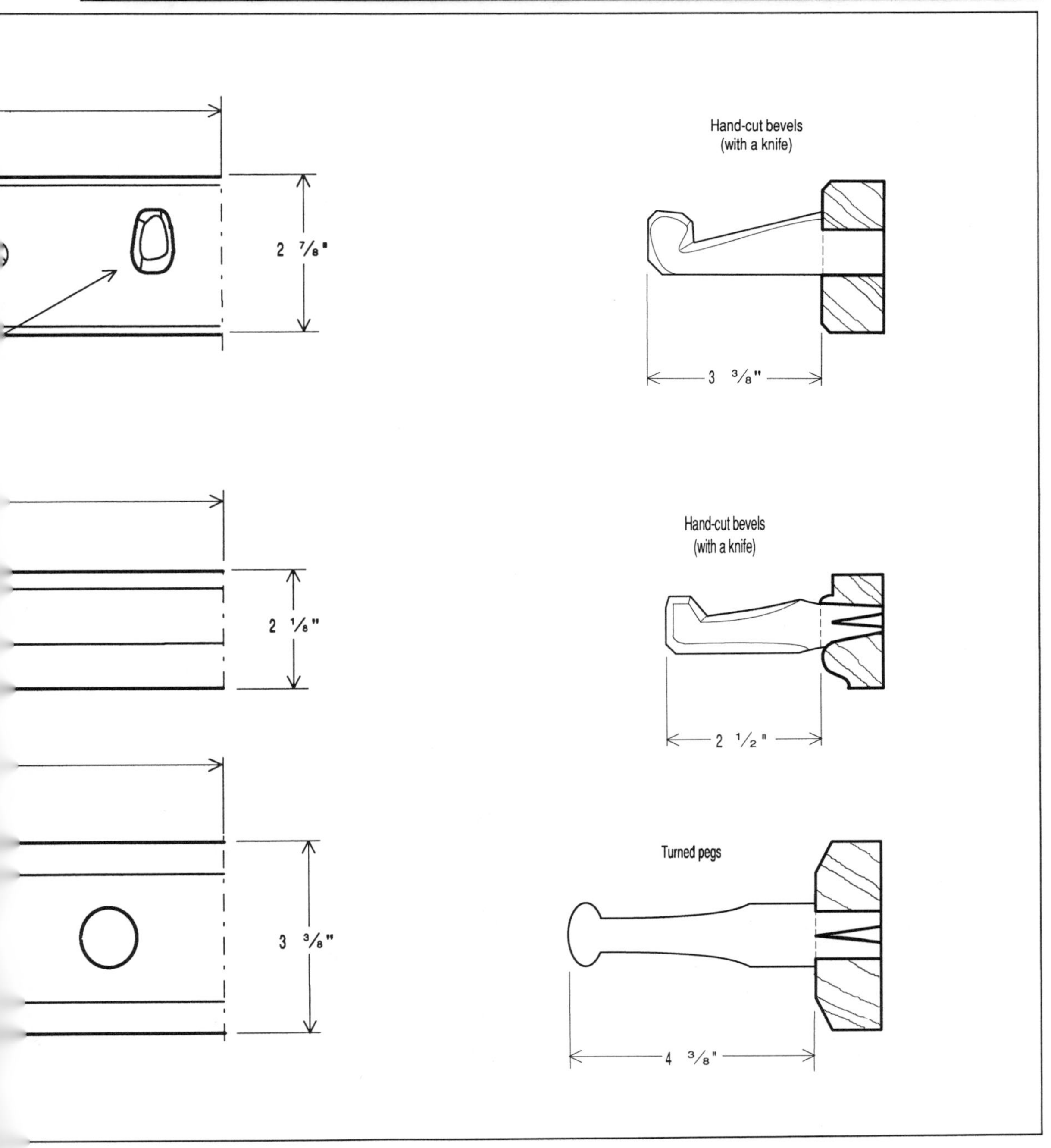

2 7/8"
Hand-cut bevels
(with a knife)
3 3/8"
2 1/8"
Hand-cut bevels
(with a knife)
2 1/2"
3 3/8"
Turned pegs
4 3/8"

INSTRUCTIONS

Easy to make

Use pine to make the peg boards. They can be fabricated in several ways. The simplest is a straight-planed strip of wood with holes for carved pegs. You can bevel the strip, or cut a molding on it. The pegs can be carved or turned. In simple boards you can attach them by making the holes in the board round while carving the tenons of the pegs with angles. Round tenons are wedged from the rear. (Use wedged tenons, and wedge perpendicular to the grain of the wood to prevent splitting.)

Brush the peg boards with a mixture of linseed oil and turpentine, or paint them with linseed oil paint.

Note: You can make these boards to any length or shape. The greater the weight they will support, the wider should be the supporting piece. But wider than 6″ should not be necessary.

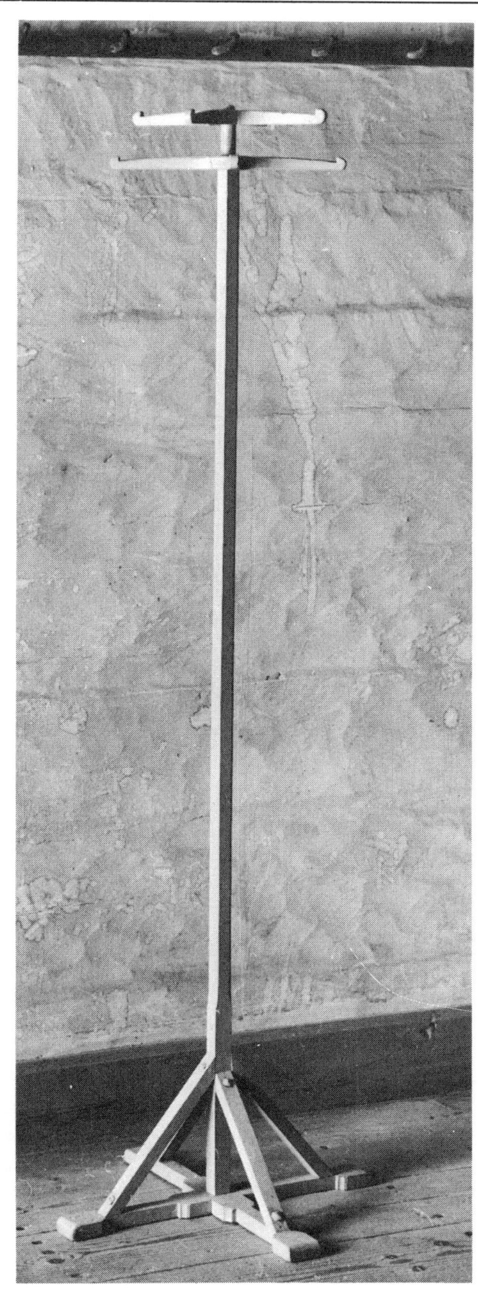

CLOTHES RACK

This free-standing pine clothes rack in Skogaholm's manor house at the Skansen exhibit is based on models from the end of the 18th century at Näs farm in Rö parish. The simple design consists of a cross-shaped foot with a pole, as well as several similar cross-shaped hangers. This type of clothes rack was common in entrance halls in the past, at least in manor houses and other residences, but very few of them have been preserved. Some of them were unpainted, others painted with linseed oil paint (like these), often in white, gray, or blue shades.

INSTRUCTIONS

Medium level of difficulty

Use pine to make this clothes rack. Plane the foot cross to 1″ × 2″, then contour as in drawing, and cut a half lap at the intersection. Drill holes for the round tenon of the pole. Plane a 70½″ long pole to 1¼″ × 1¼″, and bevel the corners. Turn the top 1¼″ of the pole to ¾″ in diameter and the 3″ section below that to a 1″ diameter.

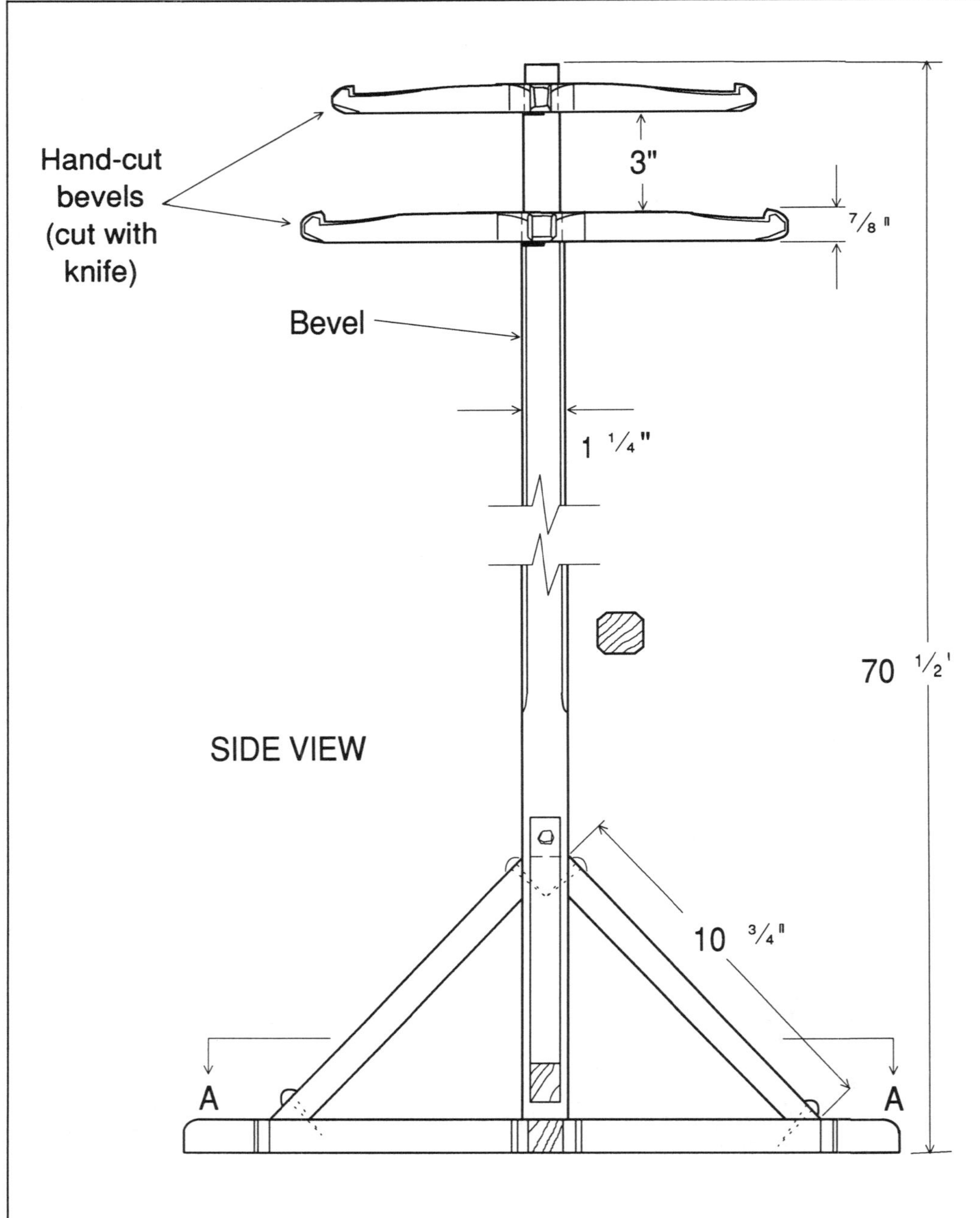

0 1 2 3 4 5 6 7 8 9 10 11 12 13 14 15 16
3/16" = 1

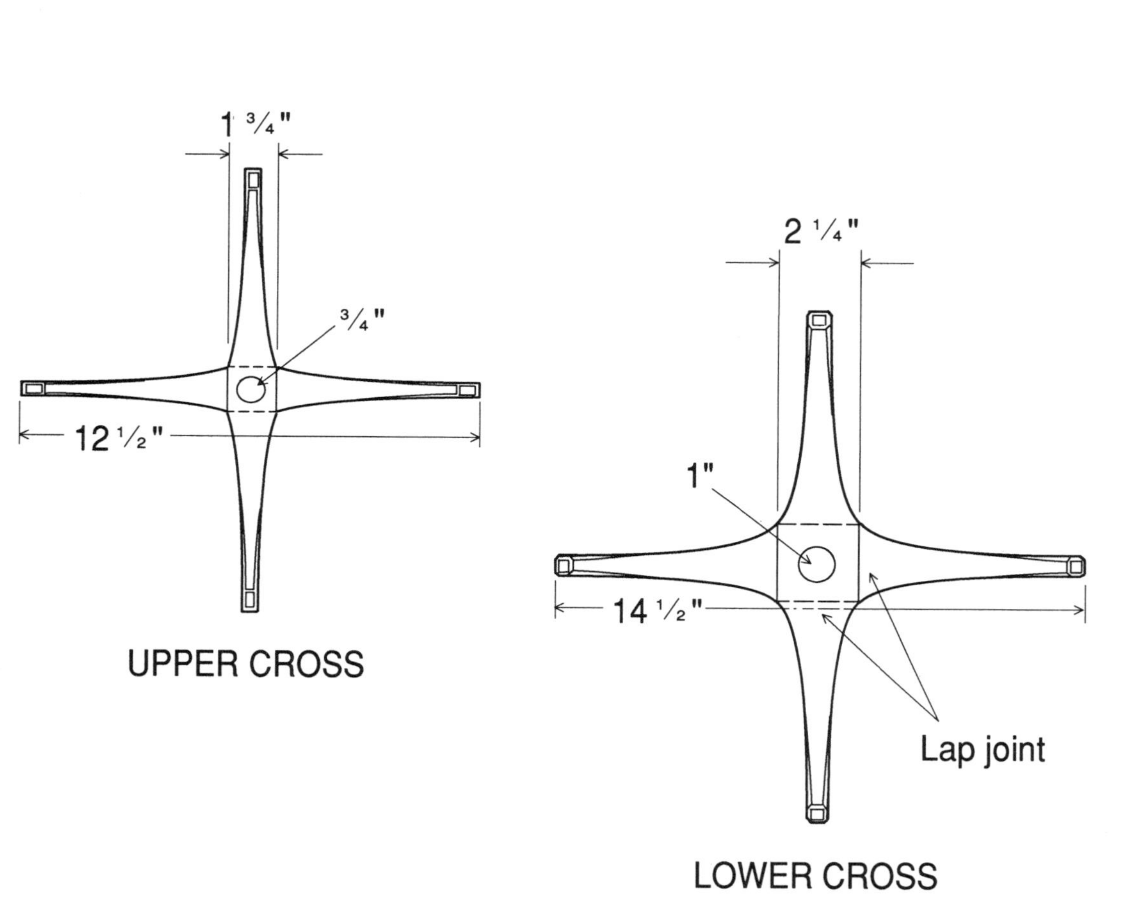
1 3/4"
3/4"
12 1/2"
UPPER CROSS
2 1/4"
1"
14 1/2"
Lap joint
LOWER CROSS

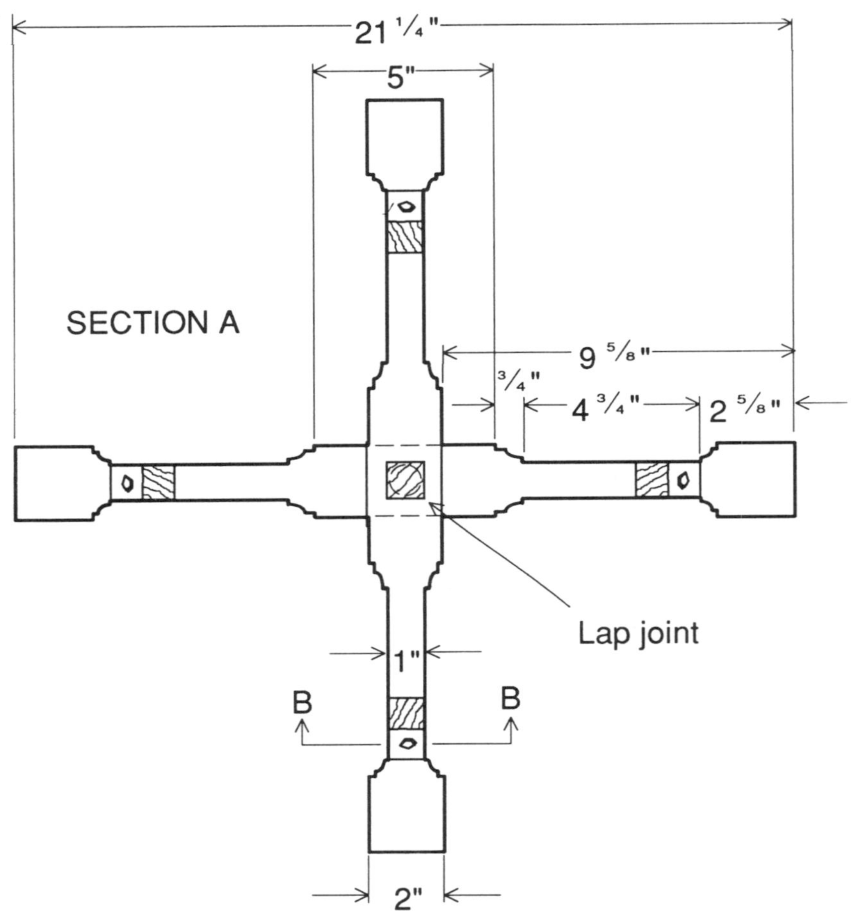

The upper and lower crosses will be slipped onto these tenons. Plane them to ⅛″ × 2¼″ and ⅞″ × 1¾″. Then saw the shape and half lap the cross at the intersection. Drill the holes to match the two different tenon dimensions. Secure the pole to the base with a 1″ wedged tenon 1″ long. Fasten angle supports with the dimensions ¾″ × 1″ to the foot and pole with nails or screws.

Paint the clothes rack with light gray linseed oil paint, a mixture of zinc white and burnt green earth.

3/16" = 1 0 1 2 3 4 5 6 7 8 9 10 11 12 13 14 15 16

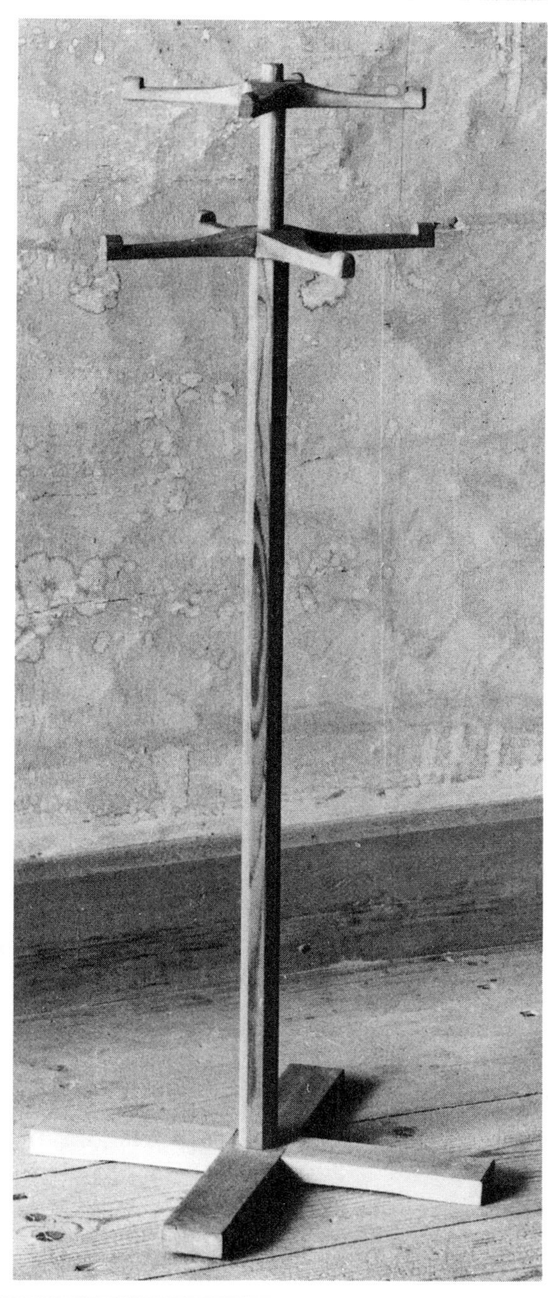

This clothes rack is also made of pine. The design is basically like that of the larger model, but the dimensions are a little smaller. The pole itself is planed to 1⅜″ × 1⅜″, and the tenons are turned to diameters of ⅞″.

Paint this clothes rack like the larger model, or brush it with a mixture of linseed oil and turpentine.

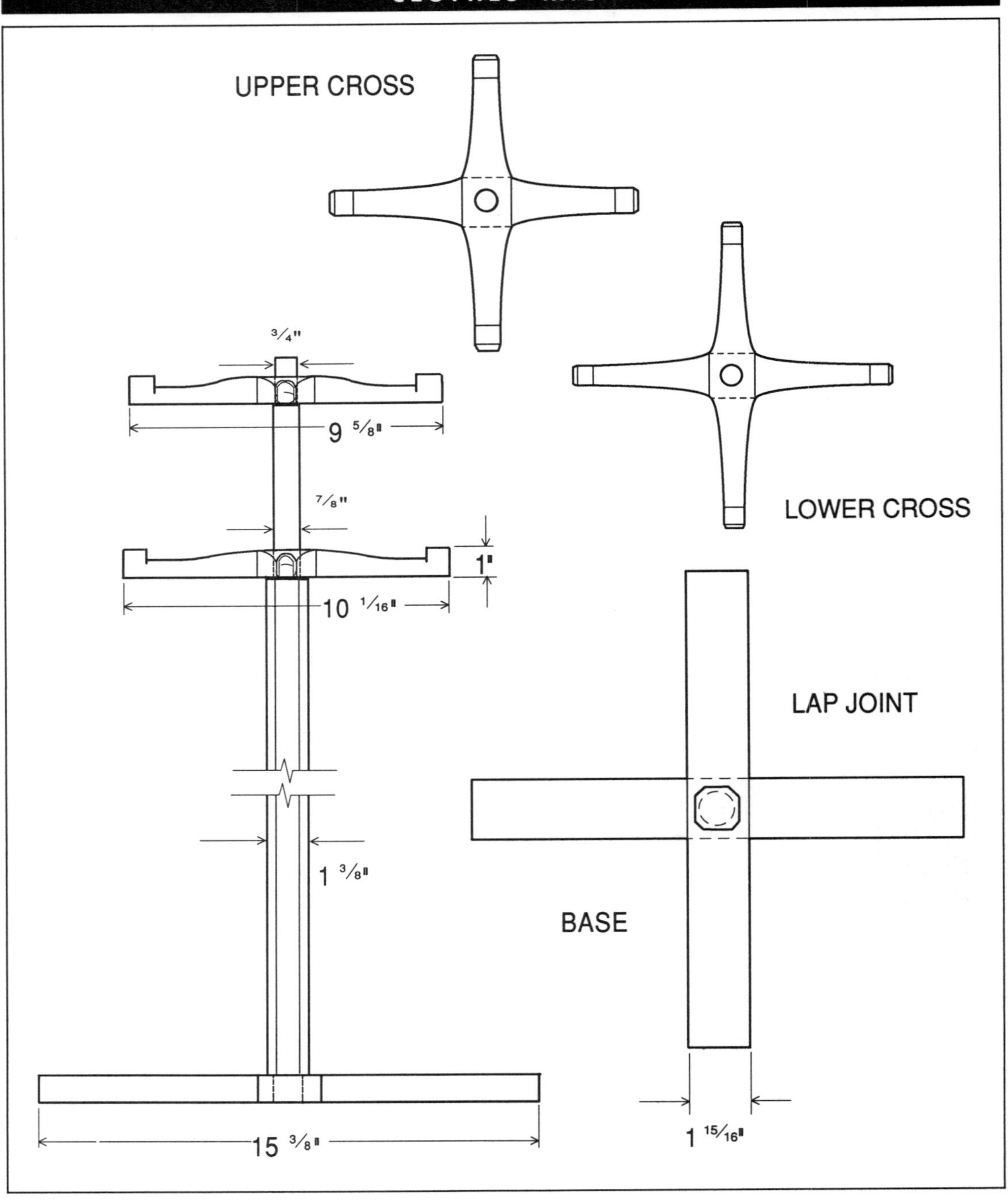

3/16" = 1
0 1 2 3 4 5 6 7 8 9 10 11 12 13 14 15 16

SMALL WALL SHELF

This small pine wall shelf for books or knickknacks is believed to have been made in Sörmland at the beginning of the 19th century. It is a simple design of three shelves with side pieces. The front edges, however, have a beveled molding, which, with its lighter red color, stands out against the other surfaces, which are painted grayish-green.

The shelf is hung on two nails through holes in the vertical brace panel on the back side.

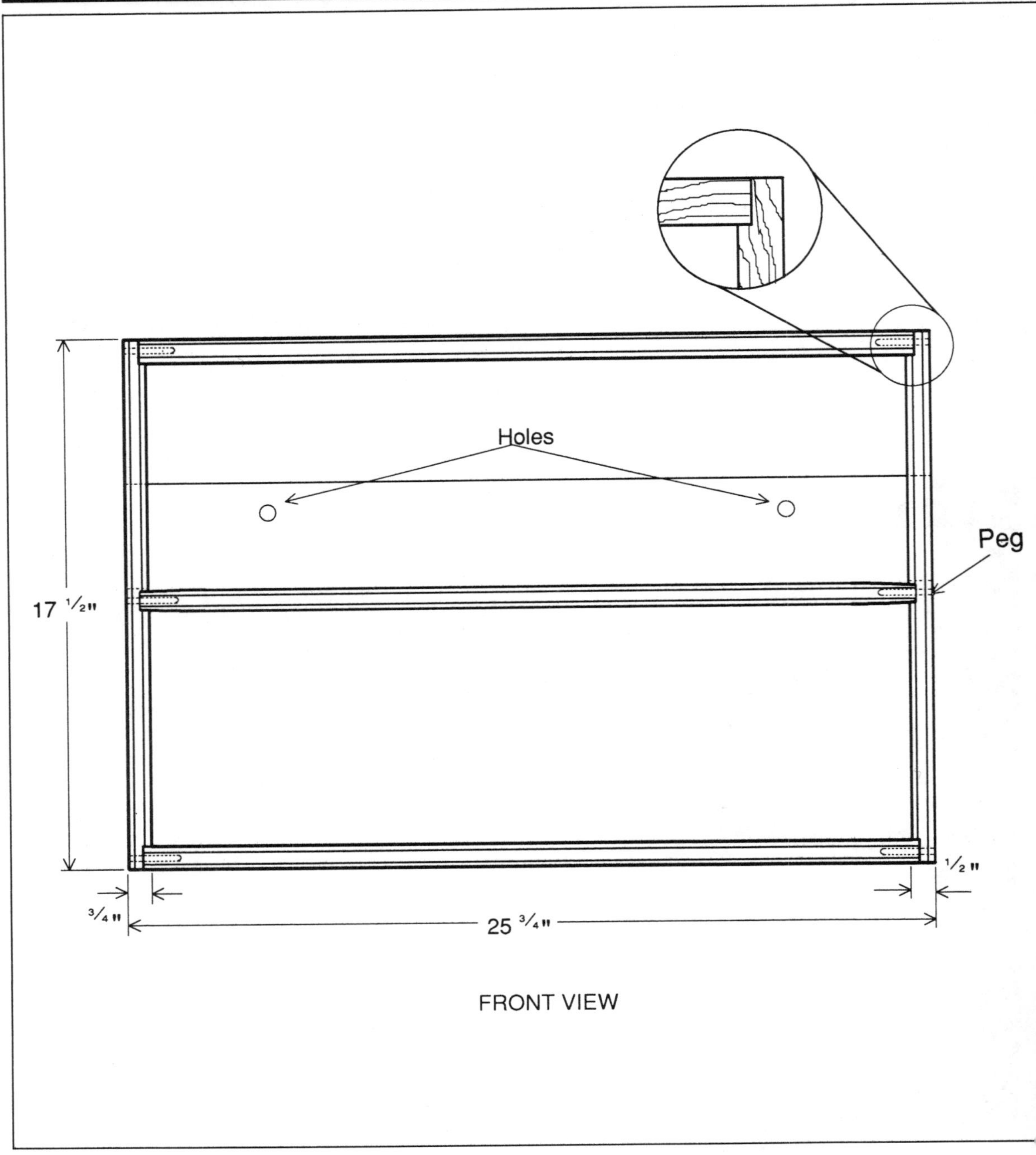

FRONT VIEW

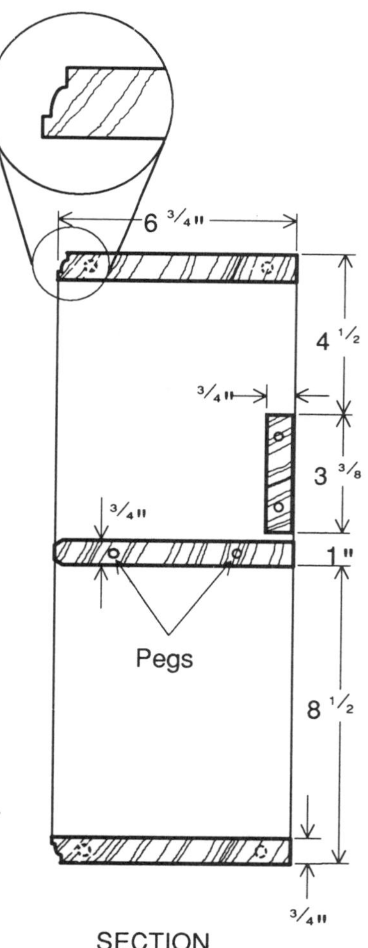

SECTION

INSTRUCTIONS

Easy to make

Use pine planed to ¾″ thick to make this shelf. The front edges of the side pieces and the upper and lower shelves have the same molding. You can make the molding with a molding plane, router, or shaper. Bevel the front edge of the center shelf. The side pieces are rabbeted with joint #6 (see Introduction) to receive the upper and lower shelves. Fasten all the shelves with dowels, with holes drilled at a slight angle.

The shelf has no back, but make a ¾″ thick panel for the back to help give the shelf stability and serve as a hanging device. This panel is rabbeted into the side pieces and fastened with dowels.

The whole unit can be assembled squarely, and drilled for doweling while clamped. Use ¼″ × 1½″ dowels with grooves to allow the glue to squeeze out.

Paint the shelf with gray linseed oil paint (a mixture of zinc white and burnt green earth). Paint the side pieces and front edges of the shelves red (Indian red or red oxide).

WALL SHELF WITH DRAWER

This pine wall shelf comes from the storeroom of "Linnéhuset" (the Linnaeus House) in Uppsala. Apparently it was originally intended for kitchen utensils (a variant of the shelves with notches and ribs for plates), but it may also have been used for books or knickknacks. The drawer which occupies the lowest shelf is also seen on plate racks starting at the end of the 18th century, especially in Uppland.

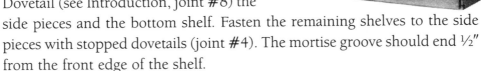

Nowadays this kind of shelf is painted with oil paint, while in the 18th century kitchen and storeroom shelves were usually unpainted. During the early part of the 19th century it became more common to paint them grayish-white or reddish-brown. The photo with empty shelves is the newly made shelf.

INSTRUCTIONS

Medium level of difficulty

Use pine to make this shelf. Plane both the side pieces and the shelves ¾″ thick. Dovetail (see Introduction, joint #8) the side pieces and the bottom shelf. Fasten the remaining shelves to the side pieces with stopped dovetails (joint #4). The mortise groove should end ½″ from the front edge of the shelf.

Continued on page 96

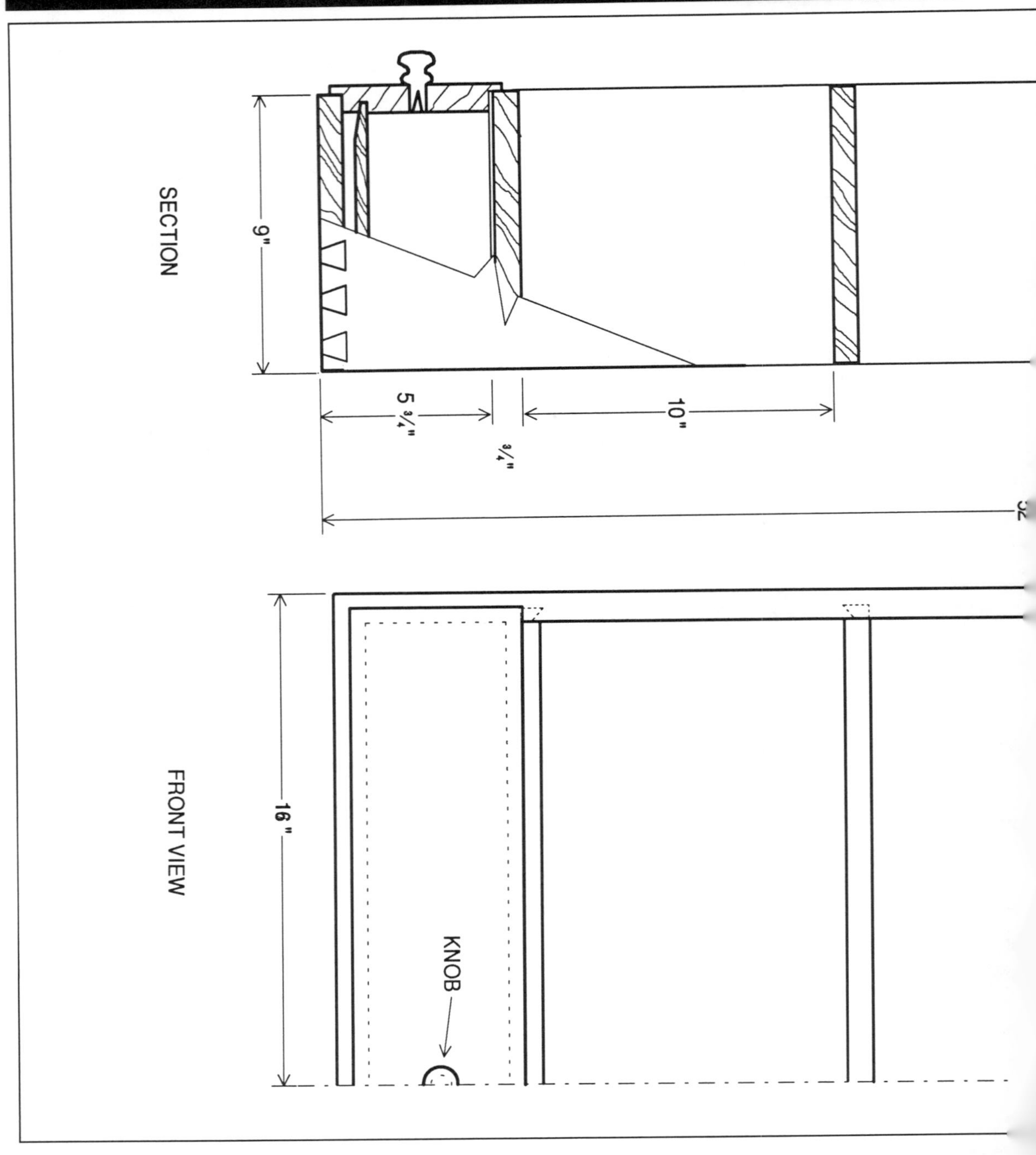

3/16" = 1 | 0 1 2 3 4 5 6 7 8 9 10 11 12 13 14 15 16

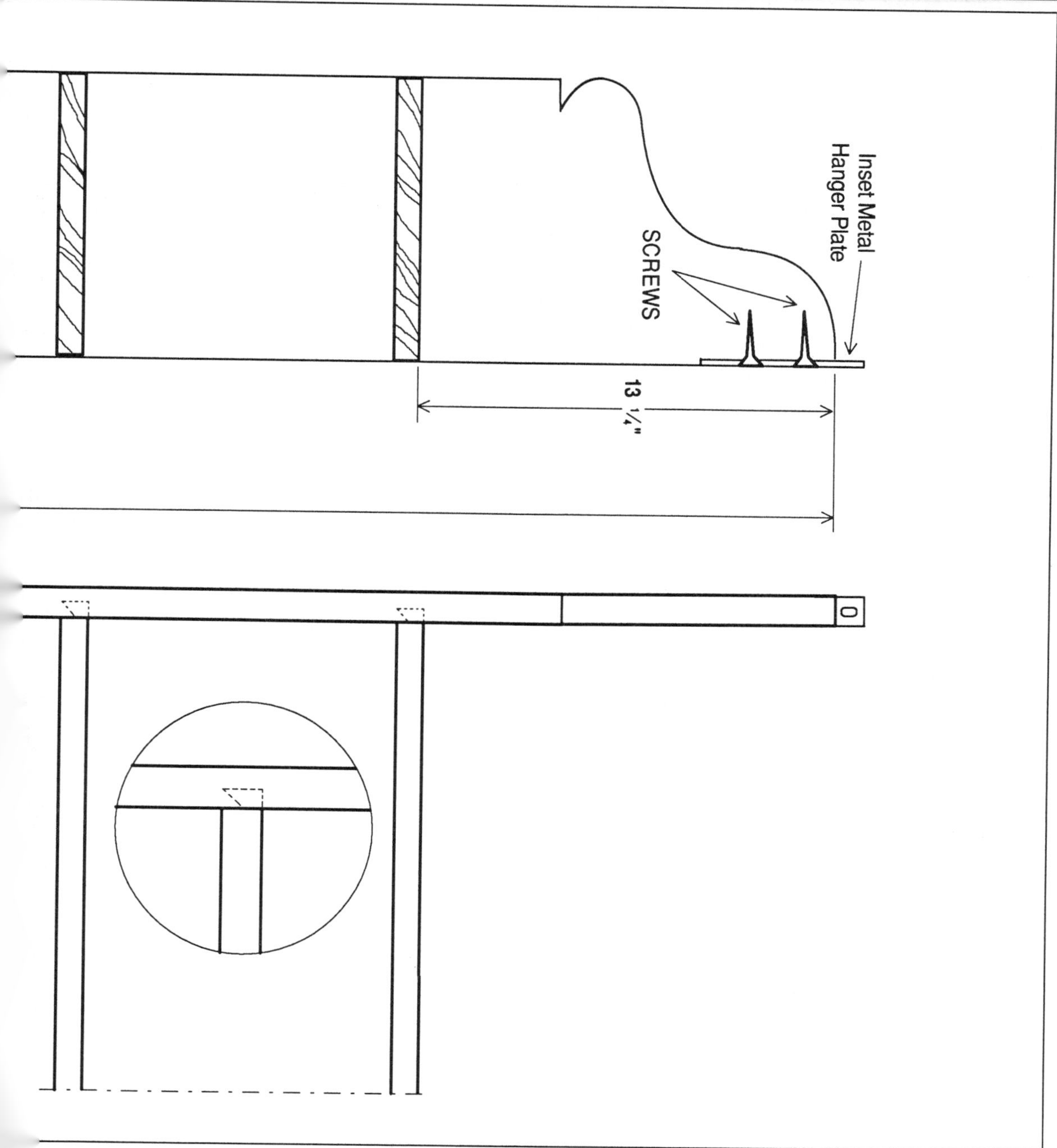
Inset Metal Hanger Plate
SCREWS
13 1/4"

Plane the front side of the drawer ¾″ thick, and rabbet it (joint #6) all the way around. Plane the side pieces, the center divider, and the back piece to a thickness of ¾″. Fasten the center divider with a rabbet (joint #1). Plane the bottom ⅜″ thick, and bevel it all the way around so it will fit into the groove. Fasten the drawer knob with a round tenon, wedged from the inside.

Traditionally this shelf is provided with forged hanging fittings which are fastened with nails or screws on the rear edges of the side pieces.

Brush the shelf with a mixture of linseed oil and turpentine, or paint it with linseed oil paint in light gray, reddish-brown, or light ochre colors.

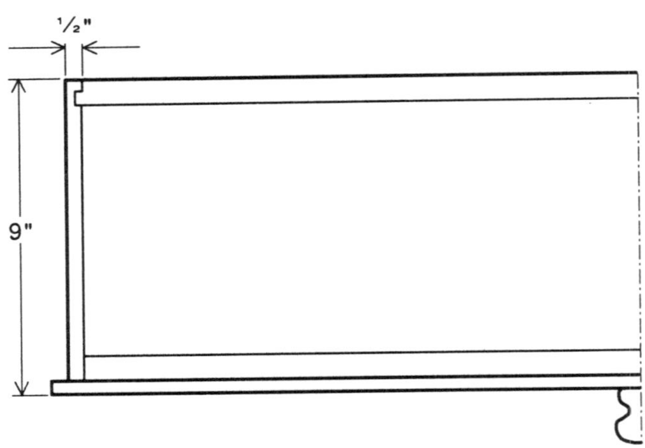

TOP VIEW OF DRAWER

3/16" = 1
0 1 2 3 4 5 6 7 8 9 10 11 12 13 14 15 16

TWO HAND-TOWEL HOLDERS

The pine hand towel holders on this page and on page 100 are from Ekshäradsgården, and Älvrosgården at the Skansen exhibit respectively. The latter is dated 1856. No ordinary hand towel racks, they were intended to hold decorative hand towels, which in the past were often found just inside the parlor door. This type of holder is shaped like a canopy with bracket-shaped side pieces and a molded front piece which encloses a top piece. The purpose of the holder, besides being a decorative framework, was to protect the hand towel from dust and soot.

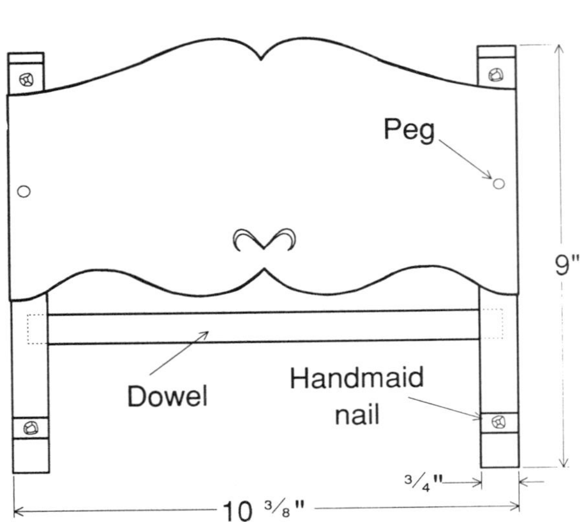

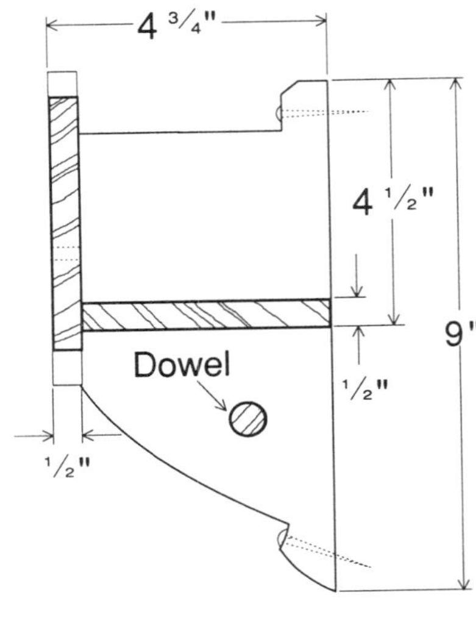

SECTION

INSTRUCTIONS

Use pine to make both these hand towel holders.

Towel holder 1. (*Easy to make.*) Plane the side pieces to a thickness of ¾", contour saw them, and provide them with a ⅝" diameter, ⅜" deep slot for the round rod. The hole must not go all the way through. Plane the front and top of the holder ½" thick. Fasten the top to the sides with a rabbet joint #1 or #2. (See Introduction.) Contour the front and fasten it to the sides with nails or wooden pegs.

The original is untreated, but the newly made piece can be brushed with a mixture of linseed oil and turpentine.

Fasten the hand towel holder to the wall with hanger fittings or screws, or provide it with fasteners similar to those used on the bracket shelves.

1/4" = 1 | 0 1 2 3 4 5 6 7 8 9 10 11 12

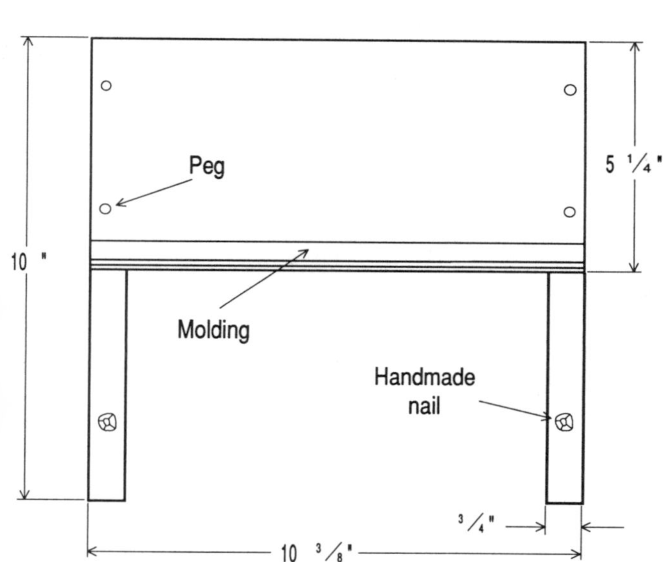

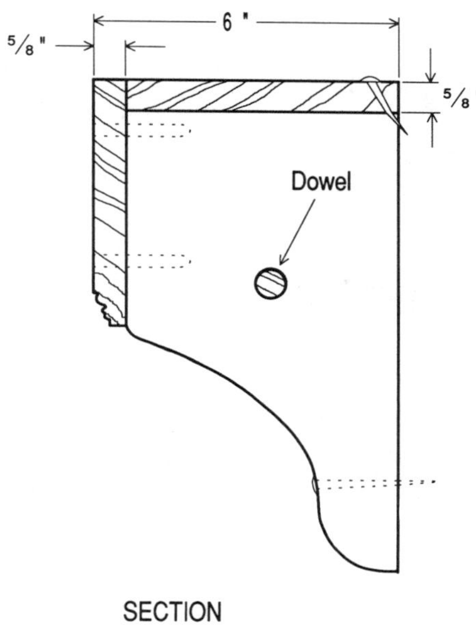

Towel holder 2. *(Slightly more difficult.)* Plane the sides, front, and top to a thickness of 5/8". Contour the sides and provide them with slots for the round rod. The slot must not go all the way through. Fasten the top and the side pieces with joint #8. (See Introduction.) Mold the lower edge of the front and fasten it with nails or wooden pegs to the side pieces.

This hand towel holder was painted with linseed oil paint in a reddish-brown mahogany color—burnt sienna.

Fasten the holder to the wall with hanger fittings or screws, or provide it with fasteners similar to those used on the bracket shelves.

1856

SINGLE PLATE SHELF

This single plate shelf, found in Morastugan at the Skansen exhibit, consists of only one shelf, low side sloping upward, with a molded support strip for the plates. It is this strip which determines the use of the shelf for plates only. Shelves of this type were most often painted in gray or reddish-brown shades with oil paints. They were usually hung as high up on the wall as possible, preferably in corners or above doorframes where they would not be in the way.

It is quite clear from the photograph on page 103, which shows the porcelain kitchen at Skogaholm's manor house at Skansen, that plate shelves were usually much more than practical items. Even in simpler settings the shelves were beautifully painted and dramatically placed.

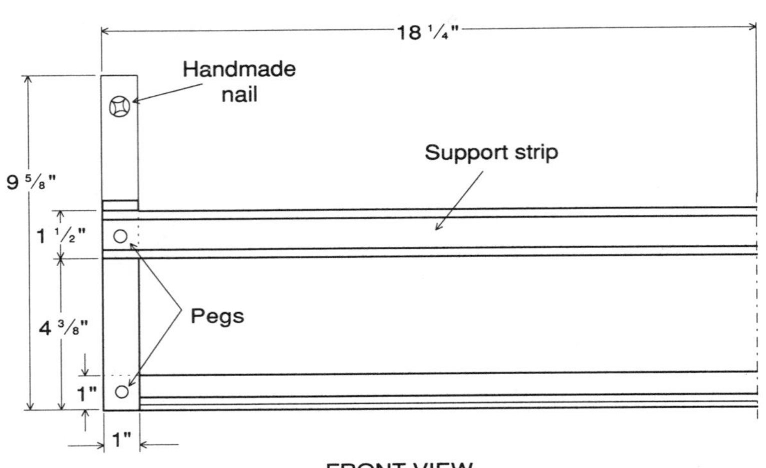

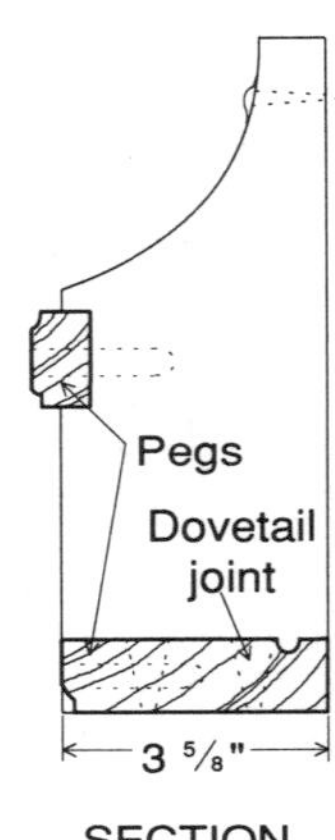

INSTRUCTIONS

Easy to make

Use pine to make this shelf. The length can be adjusted according to the space available. Plane the shelf and side pieces to a thickness of 1″. Mold the front edge of the shelf and cut a groove for plates, ⅜″ wide and ¼″ deep, approximately ½″ from the back edge of the shelf. Dovetail the corners (see Introduction, joint #8). Fasten any intermediate pieces to the shelf with two tenons locked with wooden dowels. Plane the support strip for the plates to ¾″ × 1½″ and mold it. The molding can be done with a molding plane, router, or shaper. Cut the support strip (joint #1) ⅜″ into the side pieces and fasten it with wooden pegs.

Note that lengthening the plate shelf would require pieces identical to the ends, but with through tenons attaching them to the shelf.

The plate shelf is painted with linseed oil paint, and hung up with hanger fixtures, or screwed directly into the wall.

0 1 2 3 4 5 6 7 8 9 10 11 12 13 14 15 16
3/16" = 1

DOUBLE PLATE SHELF

This double plate shelf in Älvrosgården, at the Skansen exhibit, has functional gables shaped in a rococo curve, used for the placement of the support strips and the narrow shelves. The shelf was originally painted with reddish-brown linseed oil paint.

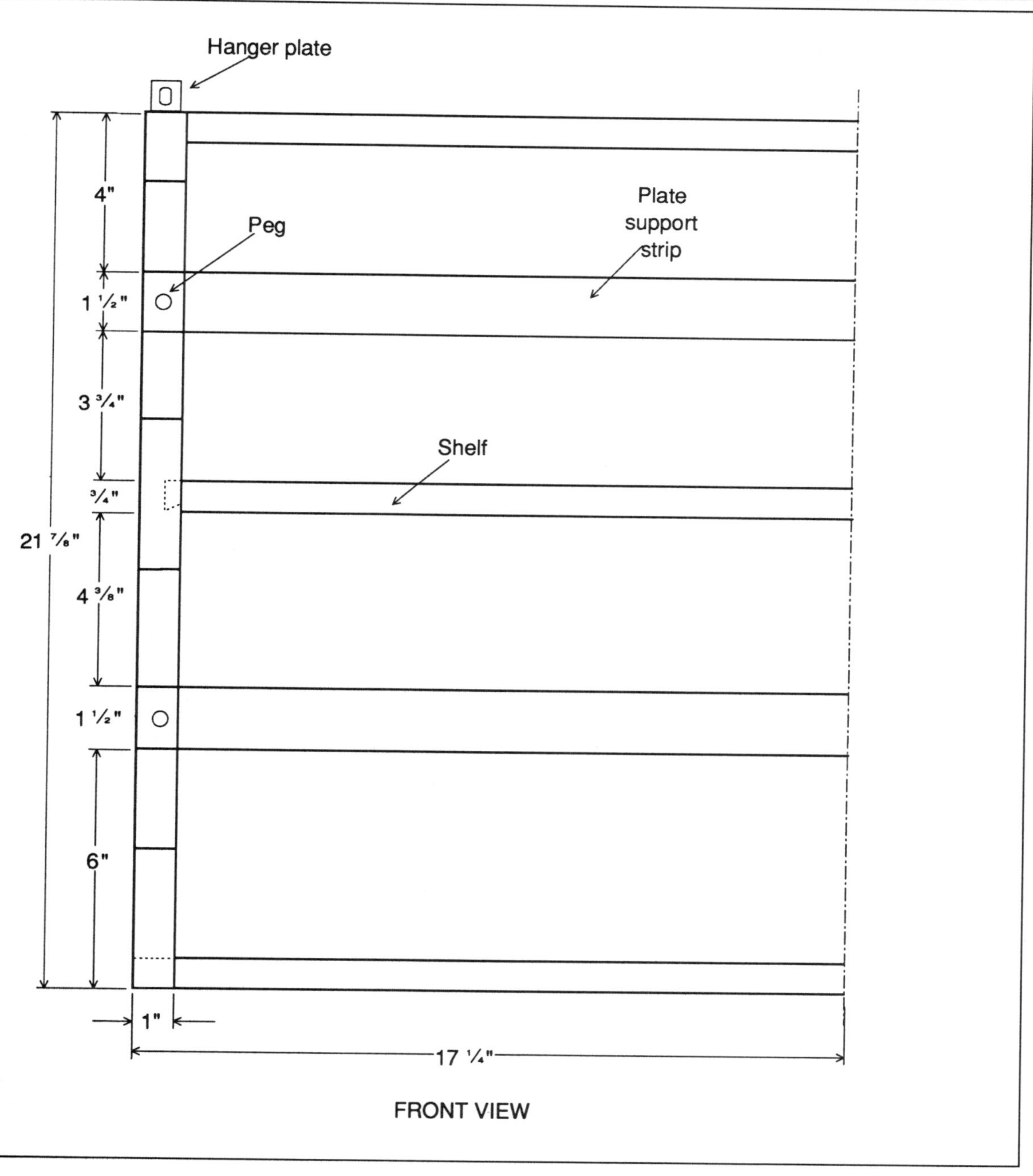
Hanger plate
Peg
Plate support strip
Shelf
4"
1 ½"
3 ¾"
¾"
21 ⅞"
4 ⅜"
1 ½"
6"
1"
17 ¼"
FRONT VIEW
1/4" = 1
0 1 2 3 4 5 6 7 8 9 10 11 12

INSTRUCTIONS

Moderate level of difficulty

Use pine to make this plate shelf. The length can be adjusted to the space available. Plane the sides 1″ thick, and contour them. Plane the shelves to a thickness of ¾″, and provide them with grooves for the plates. Attach them to the sides with dovetails (see Introduction, joint #8). Fasten the center shelf to the sides with a bare-faced dovetail (joint #2). The mortise should stop approximately ½″ inside the front edge of the shelf. Fasten any intermediate pieces to the upper and lower shelves by two through tenons locked with ¼″ wooden dowels. Plane the plate support strip to the dimensions ¾″ × 1½″, inset flush (joint #1) into the sides, and fasten it with wooden pegs.

Paint the plate shelf with linseed oil paint in a tone which complements the interior. Fasten fittings, preferably of forged flat bar steel, with holes for hanging, near the top of the back edge of the side pieces.

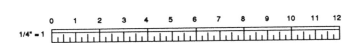

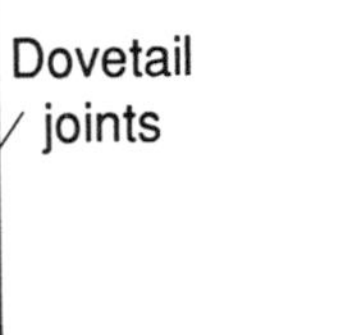

SIDE SECTION

ORNAMENT SHELF

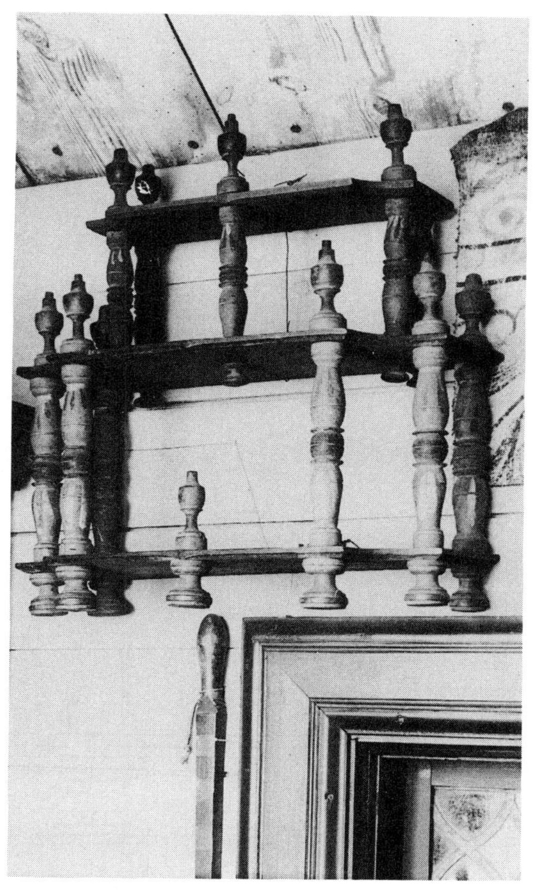

This ornament shelf ("tavelett"), originally from Hälsingland, is now atDelsbogården at the Skansen exhibit. Shelves like this one contained the few decorative objects or books in the home—psalm books, a bible, and a collection of sermons. They were either hung on the wall, or were set on cupboards and the like, in which case the knobs on the bottom served as feet. The decorative function of these shelves was emphasized by painting them in reddish-brown, and several clear colors, often blue, white, green, and red.

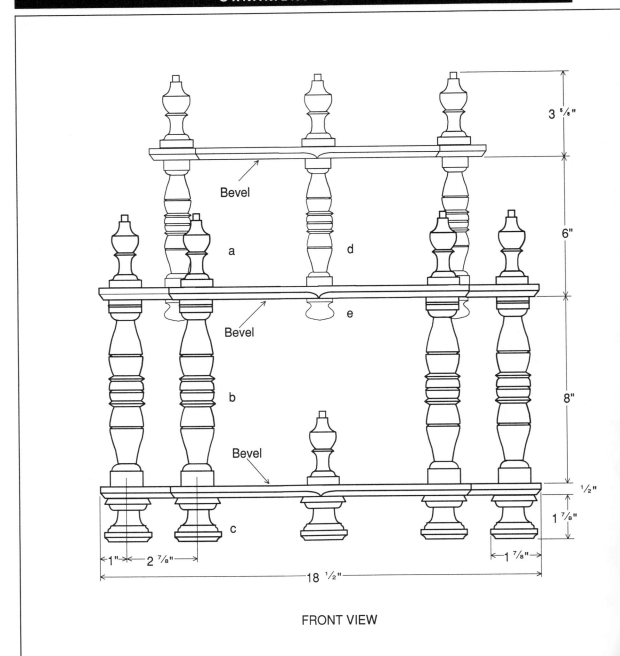

3 5/8"

Bevel

a

d

6"

e

Bevel

b

8"

Bevel

1/2"

c

1 7/8"

1" 2 7/8"

1 7/8"

18 1/2"

FRONT VIEW

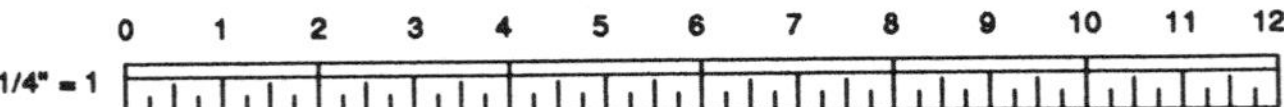

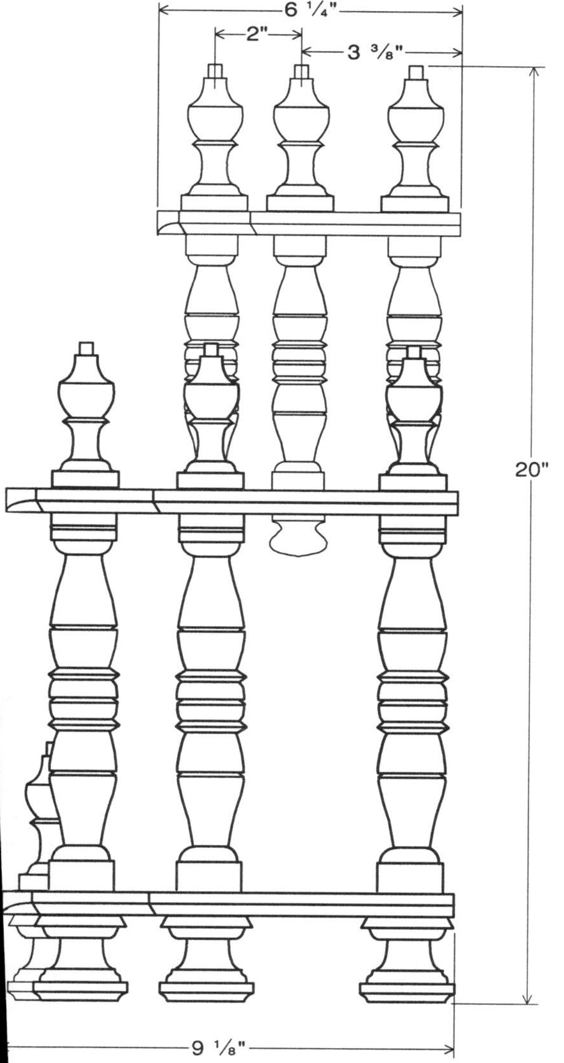

SIDE VIEW

INSTRUCTIONS

A relatively easy lathe project

Use pine to make the shelf. Plane it to a thickness of ½″, contour it, and bevel the lower edge. Turn the columns from alder or birch, and fasten them to the shelf by means of 1″ long turned tenons, which go through the shelf and into a ⅜″ hole drilled in the shorter turnings.

The "tavelett" is painted with reddish-brown linseed oil paint. The columns are decorated with red and green paint.

Hang the shelf on the wall by threading a leather thong through two holes drilled in the middle shelf. Knot the thong into a loop.

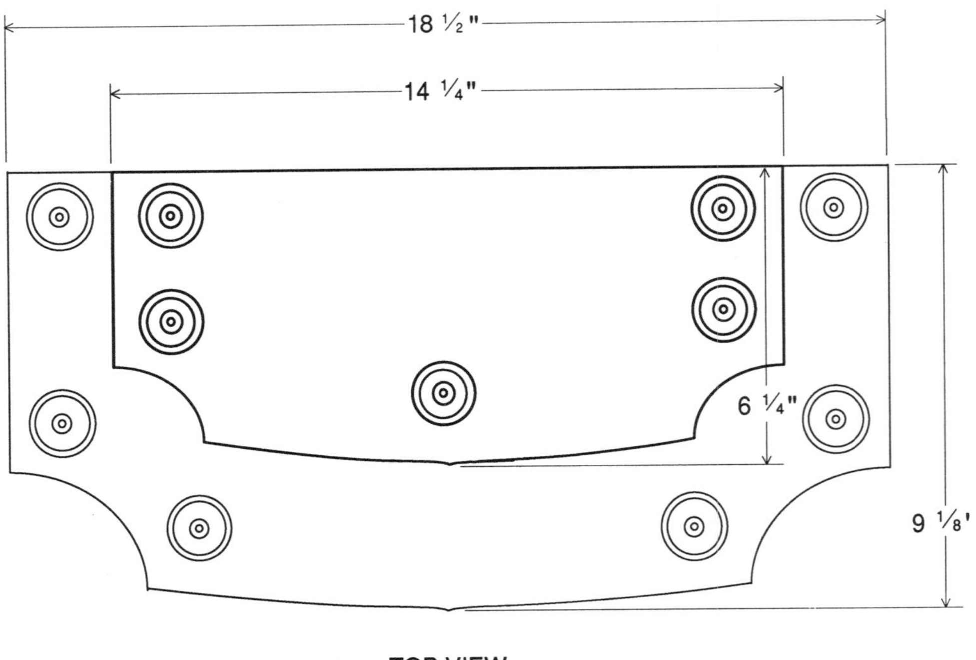

TOP VIEW

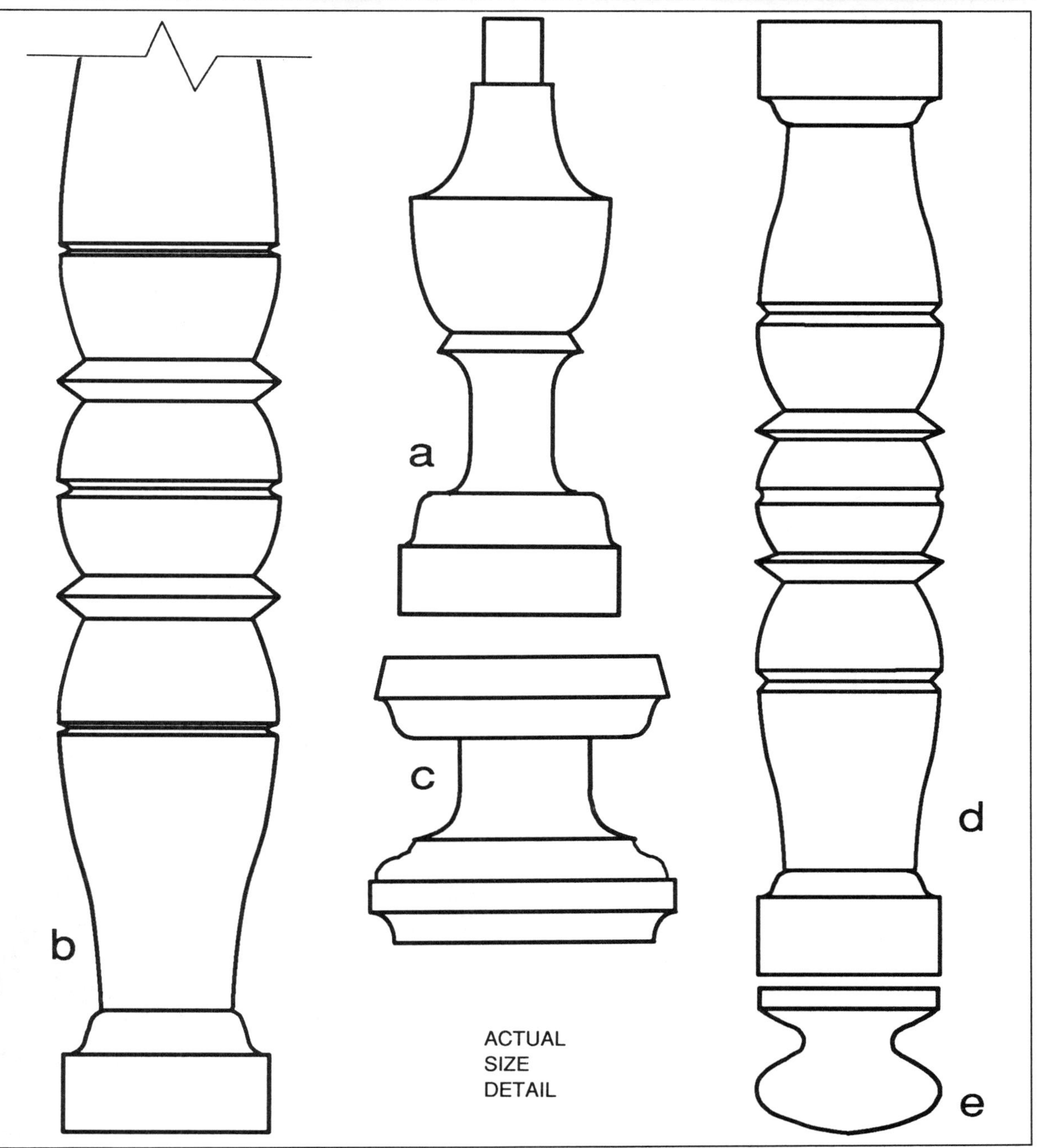
a
b
c
d
e
ACTUAL
SIZE
DETAIL

CANDLESTICK

This candlestick of wavy-grained birch is from the end of the 18th century or the beginning of the 19th. It is from Värmland, and is now at Ekshäradsgården, at Skansen. It represents a form of home woodworking in inexpensive material from a time when metals such as brass were relatively expensive. It is an old tradition in Sweden to turn candlesticks, drinking bowls, and the like in wavy grained wood or roots of alder and birch. Particularly during the latter part of the 17th century there was widespread interest in turning masur (curly-grained) birch and other wavy grained types of wood. This candlestick was turned in one piece instead of two (i.e., upright and base separately), which is the most common.

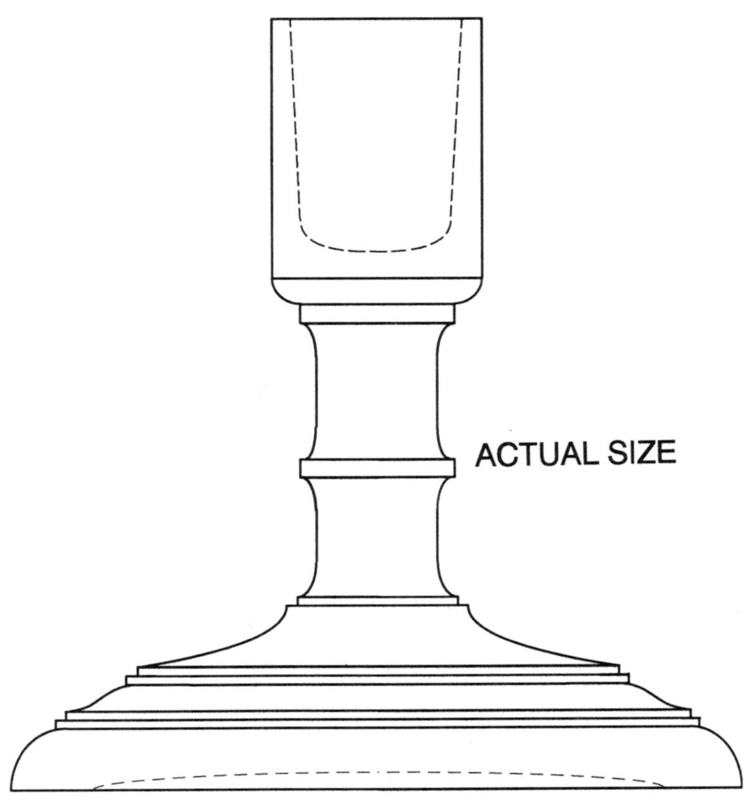

INSTRUCTIONS

Very easy to make, this lathe project would only require about 2 hours

Turn the candlestick from masur birch or another wavy grained hardwood in one piece. It will be necessary to make a pattern of the piece, then center the wood to be turned on the lathe and turn it to the desired shape. Shield the hole for the candle with a cuff of sheet metal with a bottom. The candlestick that was the original model for the measurements was completely untreated. The newly made candlestick may be brushed with a mixture of linseed oil and turpentine.

FOUR-ARMED CHANDELIER

This pine chandelier from Hälsingland is now in Delsbogården at the Skansen exhibit. This simple, surely very ancient unpainted type of chandelier was probably first used at Christmas time and for other major holidays. It consists of four crossbeams supported by a square center column by which it hangs from the ceiling.

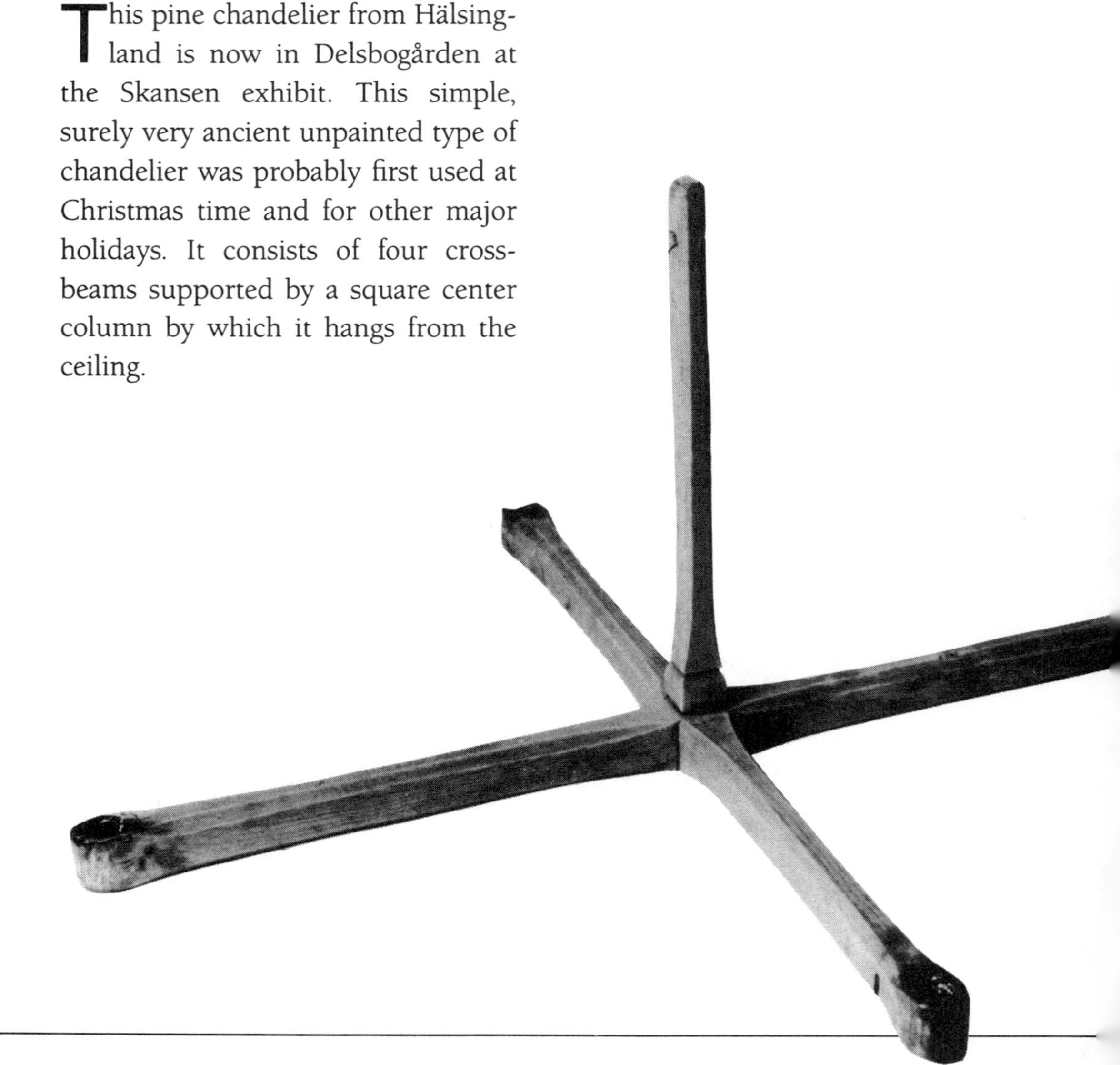

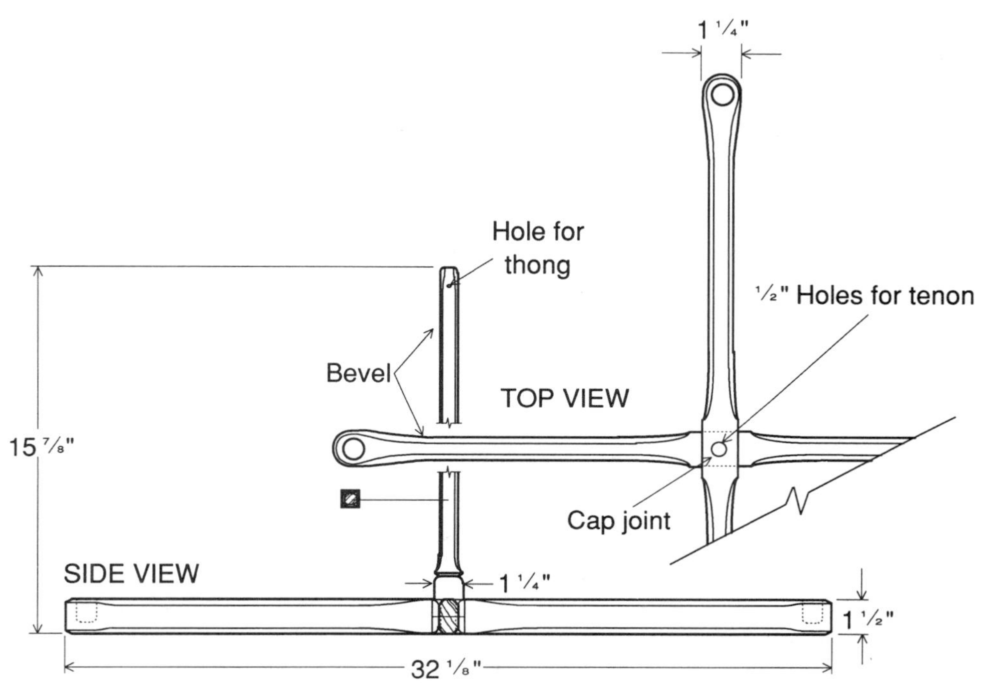

INSTRUCTIONS

Very easy to make

Use pine to make this chandelier. Mark out the arms and center post, and use a rasp for the finished shape. Shape the center column from a 1¼″ × 1¼″ piece, and at the top drill a small hole for the hanger. Shape the arms from a 1¼″ × 1½″ piece. The arms are half lapped (see Introduction, joint #7) at the intersection, and a hole is drilled for the tenon of the center column, which is wedged. Drill holes for the candles and shield them with cuffs made of sheet metal. The cuffs must have a bottom.

The chandelier may be left untreated or brushed with a mixture of linseed oil and turpentine.

1/8" = 1 | 0 2 4 6 8 10 12 14 16 18 20 22 24

SIX-ARMED CHANDELIER

This six-armed chandelier from Bergslagen is now in Bergmansgården at the Skansen exhibit. While it was inspired by the bronze chandeliers of the baroque period, this chandelier is made of turned and contoured wood, and is painted with a grayish-white oil paint. Chandeliers of this type, with a turned center column and arms of wood or wrought iron, were made for both churches and residences during the 17th and 18th centuries as substitutes for cast bronze or brass chandeliers.

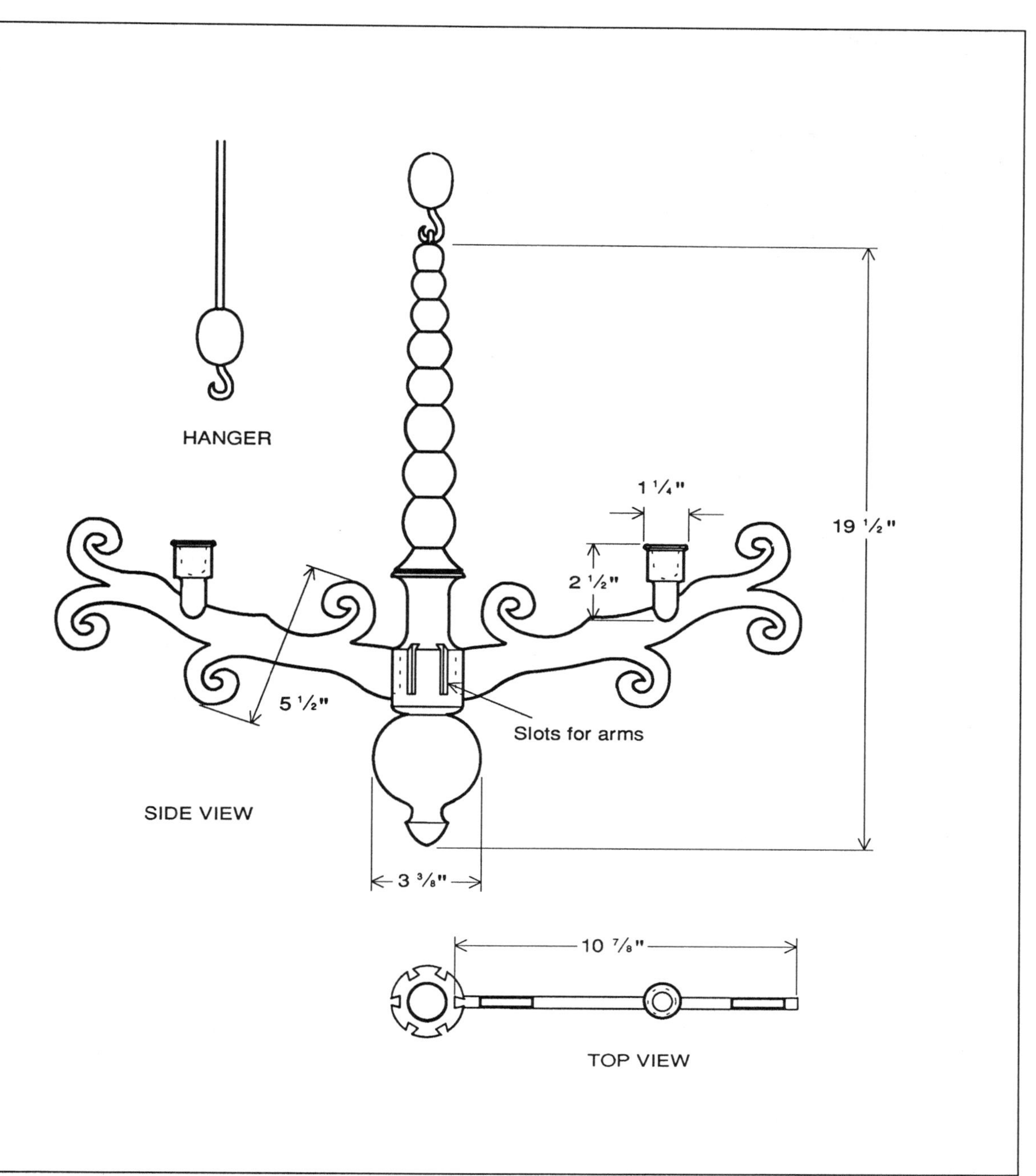
HANGER
1 ¼"
19 ½"
2 ½"
5 ½"
Slots for arms
SIDE VIEW
3 ⅜"
10 ⅞"
TOP VIEW
0 1 2 3 4 5 6 7 8 9 10 11 12 13 14 15 16
3/16" = 1

INSTRUCTIONS

Medium level of difficulty

Use a hardwood to make this chandelier. Turn the center column in one piece. Cut slots in the cylindrical section for the arms. Plane the arms to a thickness of 3⁄8″, contour them, and fasten them with a stopped dovetail (see Introduction, joint #4). Then cut slots to fasten the candleholders onto the arms. Sheet metal candle cuffs with bottoms are provided to protect against fire.

Hang the chandelier from the ceiling with the appropriate number of hangers with hooks and turned wooden balls. The hangers are made from square steel or 1⁄4″ rod.

Paint the chandelier with linseed oil paint in a light gray color—a mixture of zinc white and burnt green earth. Both hangers and candle cuffs are oil-burned. Do this by heating the iron fixture over an open fire (preferably outdoors to avoid the choking odor of burned linseed oil). Then apply a thin coat of linseed oil with a rag. Repeat the treatment and wipe dry with a dry rag. One way to finish the iron is to brush it with some beeswax dissolved in turpentine.

SMALL WALL MIRROR

This small pine wall mirror is in the pensioner's cottage of Delsbogården at the Skansen exhibit. It consists of a molded frame with a contoured, forward-leaning crest. The mirror appears to have been gilded at one time. The frame has chalk priming underneath the oil paint, a technique commonly used for gilding. Whether this mirror was made only as a wall mirror, or whether it once had a fold-out prop, is unclear. Small mirrors of this type from the end of the 18th century and the beginning of the 19th century may indeed have props such as in the somewhat larger model on page 122.

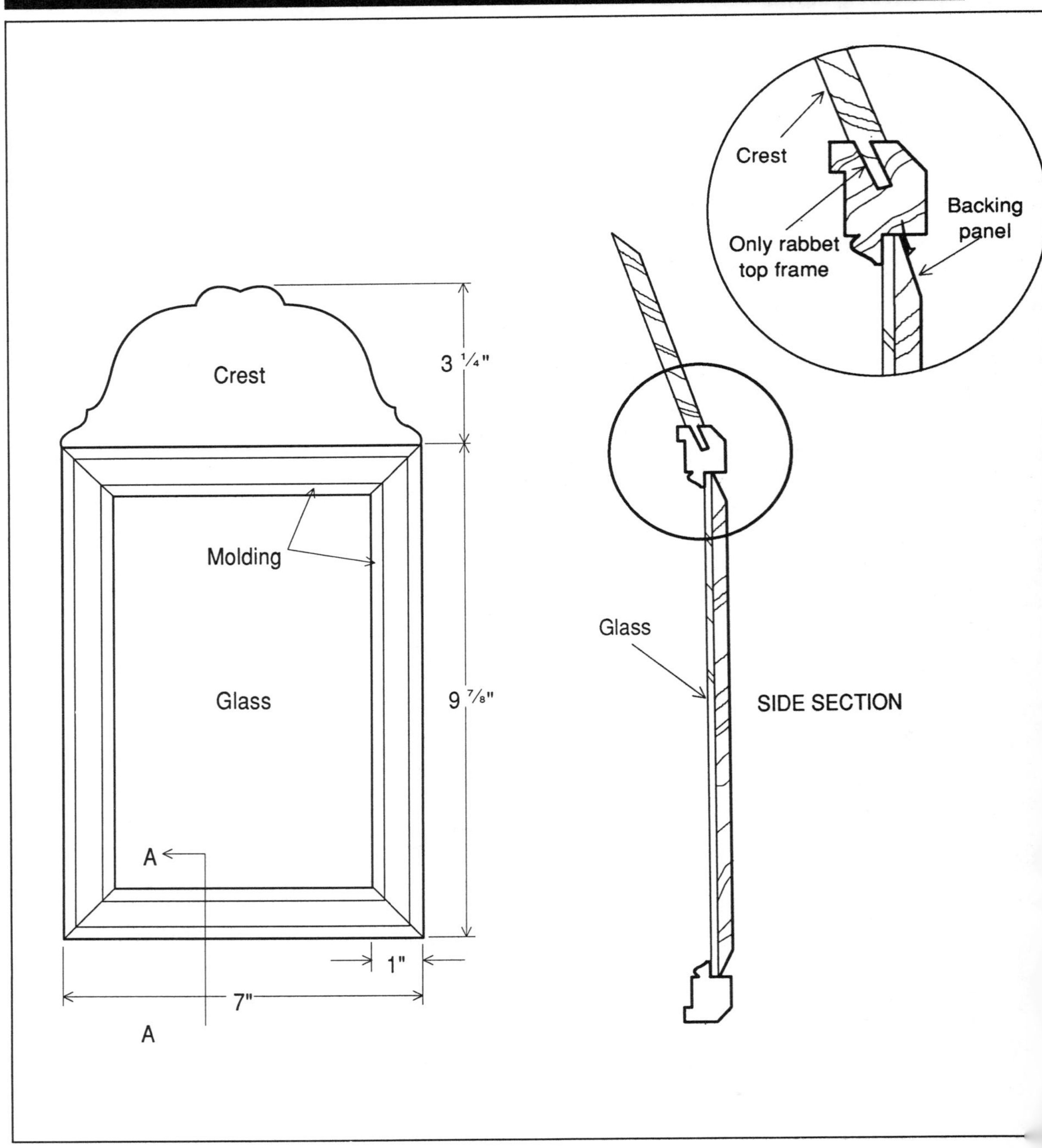
Crest
3 1/4"
Molding
Glass
9 7/8"
A
1"
7"
A
Crest
Only rabbet top frame
Backing panel
Glass
SIDE SECTION

0 1 2 3 4 5 6 7 8 9
5/16" = 1

INSTRUCTIONS

Relatively easy to make

Use pine to make this mirror. Mold the frame and miter the corners. Glue it together and brad nail the corners. Plane the crest of the mirror to a thickness of 3⁄8″, contour it, and bevel it along the entire rear edge. Join it to the top of the frame with a rabbet, or glue it directly to the top of the frame.

Hold the glass in place by nailing a planed wooden panel to the back of the frame. This mirror can also have a prop. If you wish to add one, make it in the same manner as the one for the large mirror which follows, but reduce its dimensions.

The front and sides of the original frame are chalk-primed, but only the front is gilded (see Priming and Gilding, in the Introduction). The outer molding of the frame and the crest are covered with genuine gold leaf. This is applied after the chalk primer has been brushed with red gilding paste. The other parts of the frame are coated with composition gold leaf directly onto the chalk primer. The rest of the frame is unfinished.

MIRROR

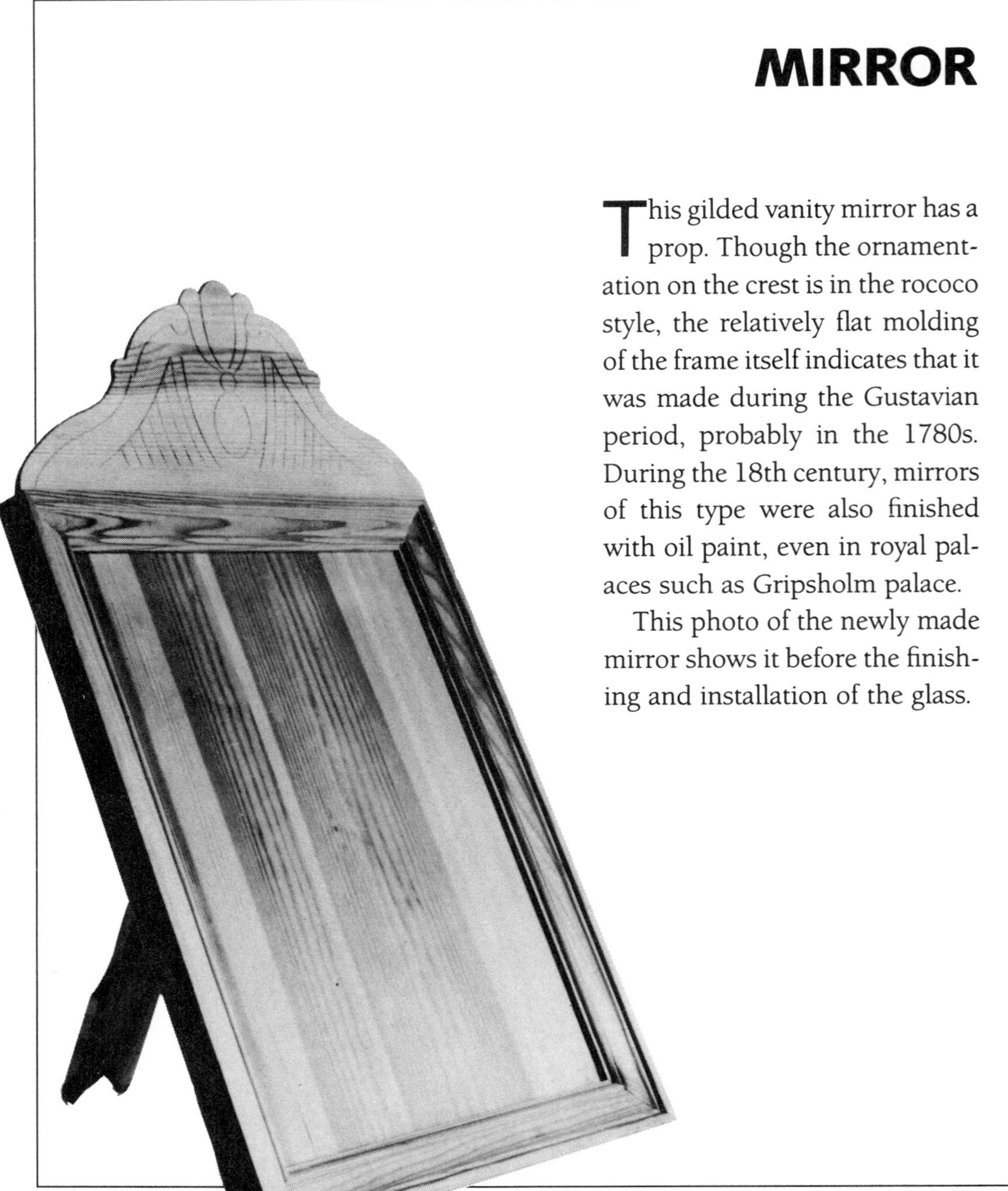

This gilded vanity mirror has a prop. Though the ornamentation on the crest is in the rococo style, the relatively flat molding of the frame itself indicates that it was made during the Gustavian period, probably in the 1780s. During the 18th century, mirrors of this type were also finished with oil paint, even in royal palaces such as Gripsholm palace.

This photo of the newly made mirror shows it before the finishing and installation of the glass.

INSTRUCTIONS

Moderately easy to medium level of difficulty

Use pine to make this mirror frame. Mold the frame and bevel it at the corners. Put it together with splines glued into the corners. Plane the crest of the mirror to a thickness of 3⁄8″, contour it, and bevel it along the entire rear edge. Plane the lower edge to 77°, and glue it to the top of the frame.

Hold the glass in place with a 1⁄4″ planed wooden panel nailed to the back of the frame. Plane the leg and crossbar to a thickness of 3⁄8″, and plane the leg down to only 1⁄4″ at the foot. Connect the crossbar and leg with a half lap (see Introduction, joint #7). Carve the round tenons in the crossbar. Fit the crossbar into the wooden blocks that are drilled and glued to the back of the mirror. Bevel the crossbar's top edge to stop against the back panel.

The front and sides of the original mirror are chalk-primed (see Priming and Gilding, in the Introduction) but only the front is gilded. The outer molding of the frame and crest, and the stylized flower of the crest, are gilded with genuine gold leaf, which is applied after the chalk primer is brushed with red gilding paste. The gold is later polished with an agate. The other parts of the frame and the front of the crest are coated with composition (imitation) gold leaf directly onto the chalk primer. The rest of the frame is unfinished. The mirror glass of the original has a 3⁄4″ wide beveled edge.

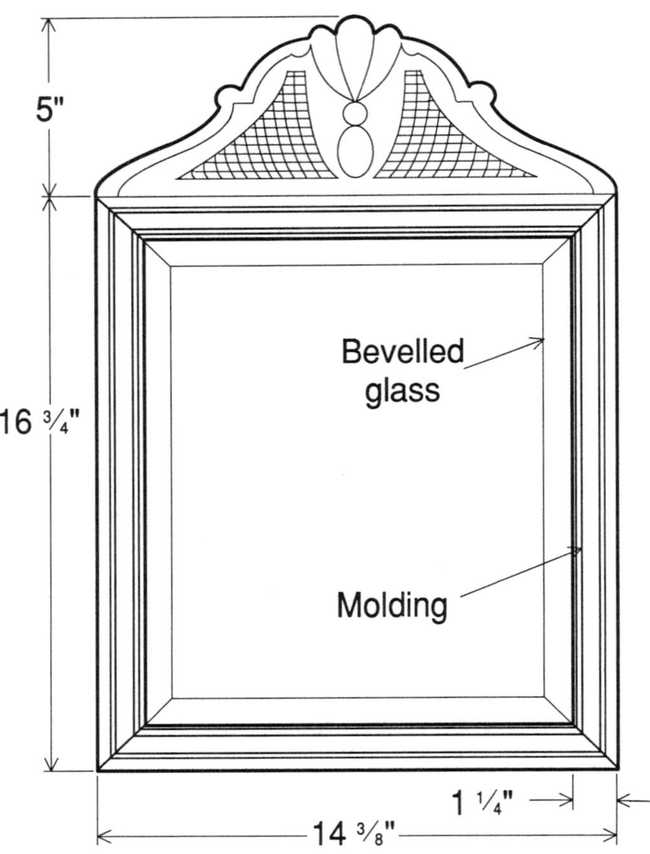

FRONT VIEW

0 1 2 3 4 5 6 7 8 9 10 11 12 13 14 15 16
3/16" = 1

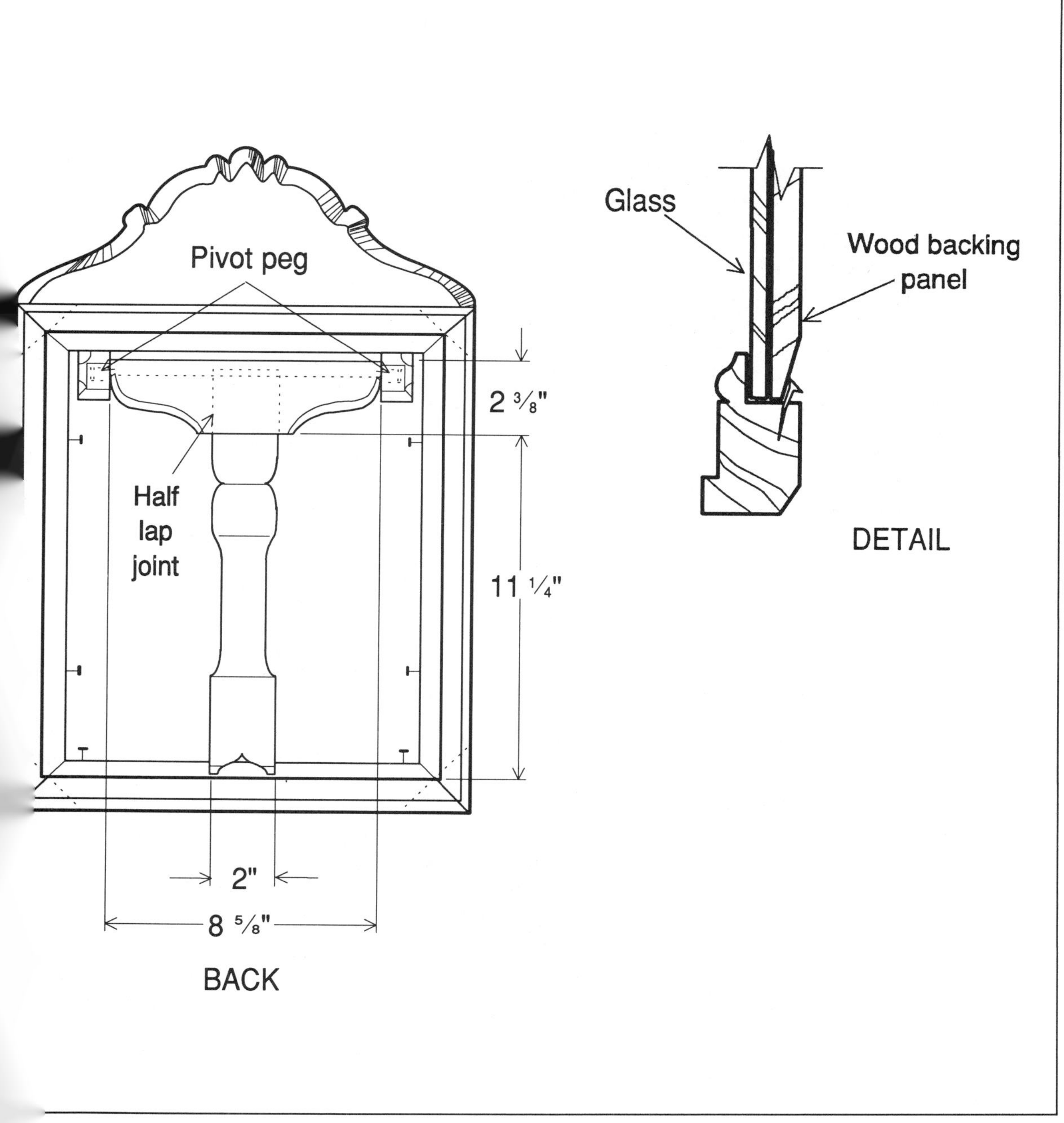

Pivot peg
Half lap joint
2 3/8"
11 1/4"
2"
8 5/8"
BACK
Glass
Wood backing panel
DETAIL

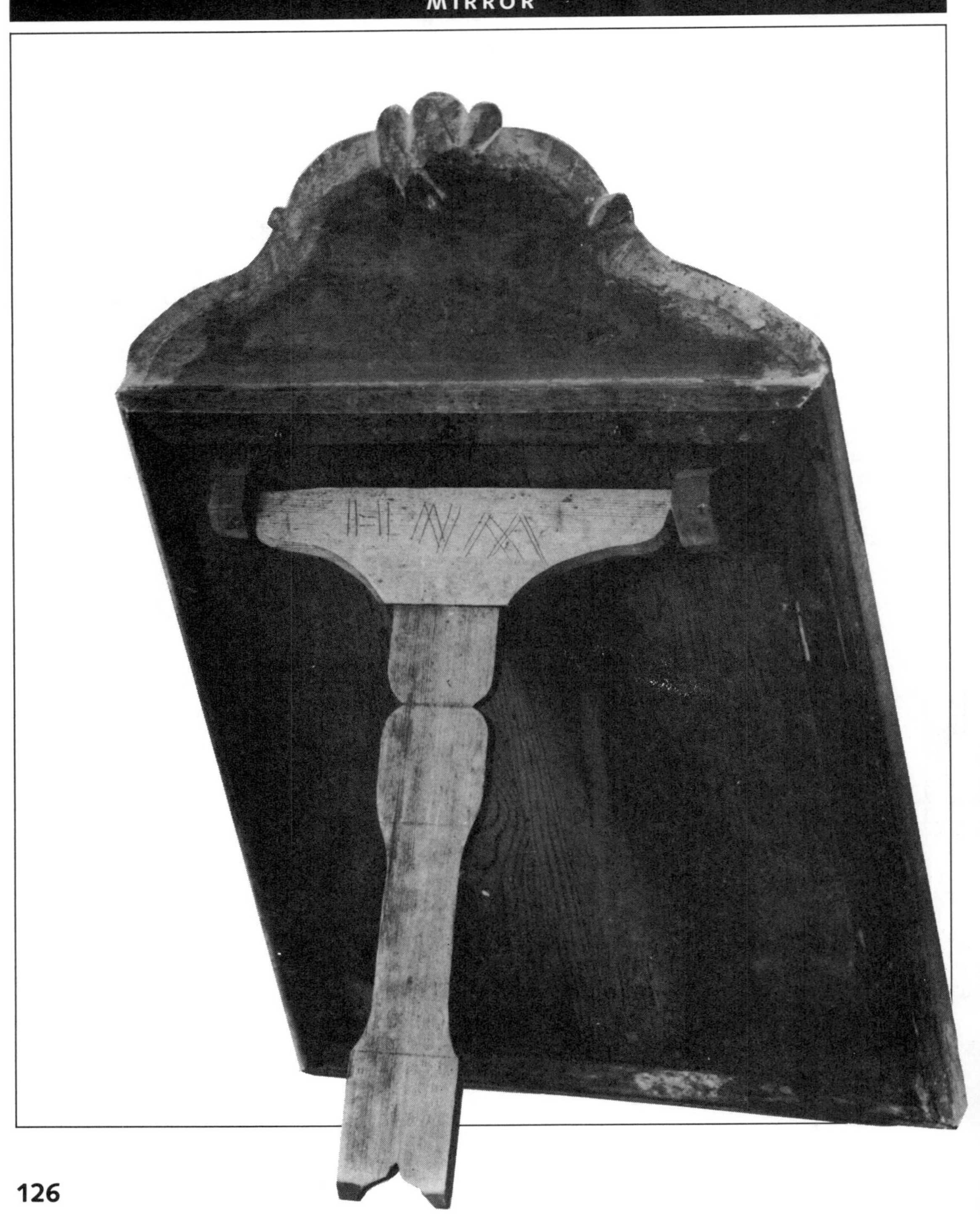

JEWELRY BOX

This small pine and oak jewelry box is from Husby Långhundra parish, in Uppland. It was probably made in the 1840s or 1850s, and was painted a reddish-brown color, which was supposed to imitate fine hardwood. This type of box, with its desk-like shape, was used for storing writing materials or jewelry. Such jewelry boxes were often called "sweetheart boxes," and were often finished with decorative painting on the outside.

The lid of the box has strips along the front and sides, and a homemade hinge, which is nailed on the inside of the lid and the back side of the box.

The box's original lock, which has disappeared, was set into the front panel.

The second, lighter box of the same type (see page 131) was made in the 18th century in Västergötland. It is made of oak, and is unpainted.

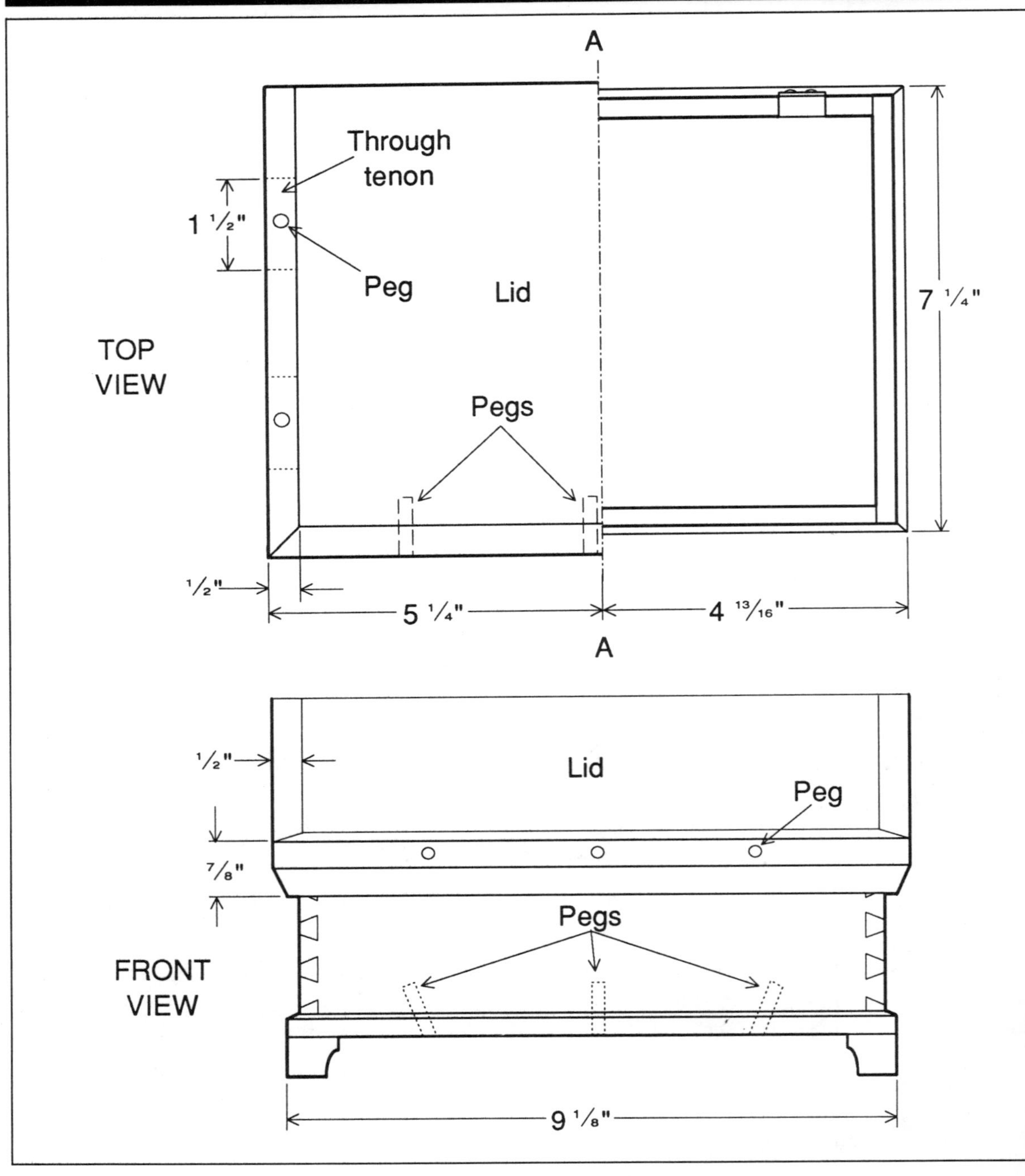
A
Through tenon
1 1/2"
Peg
Lid
7 1/4"
TOP VIEW
Pegs
1/2"
5 1/4"
4 13/16"
A
1/2"
Lid
Peg
7/8"
Pegs
FRONT VIEW
9 1/8"
0 1 2 3 4 5 6 7 8
3/8" = 1

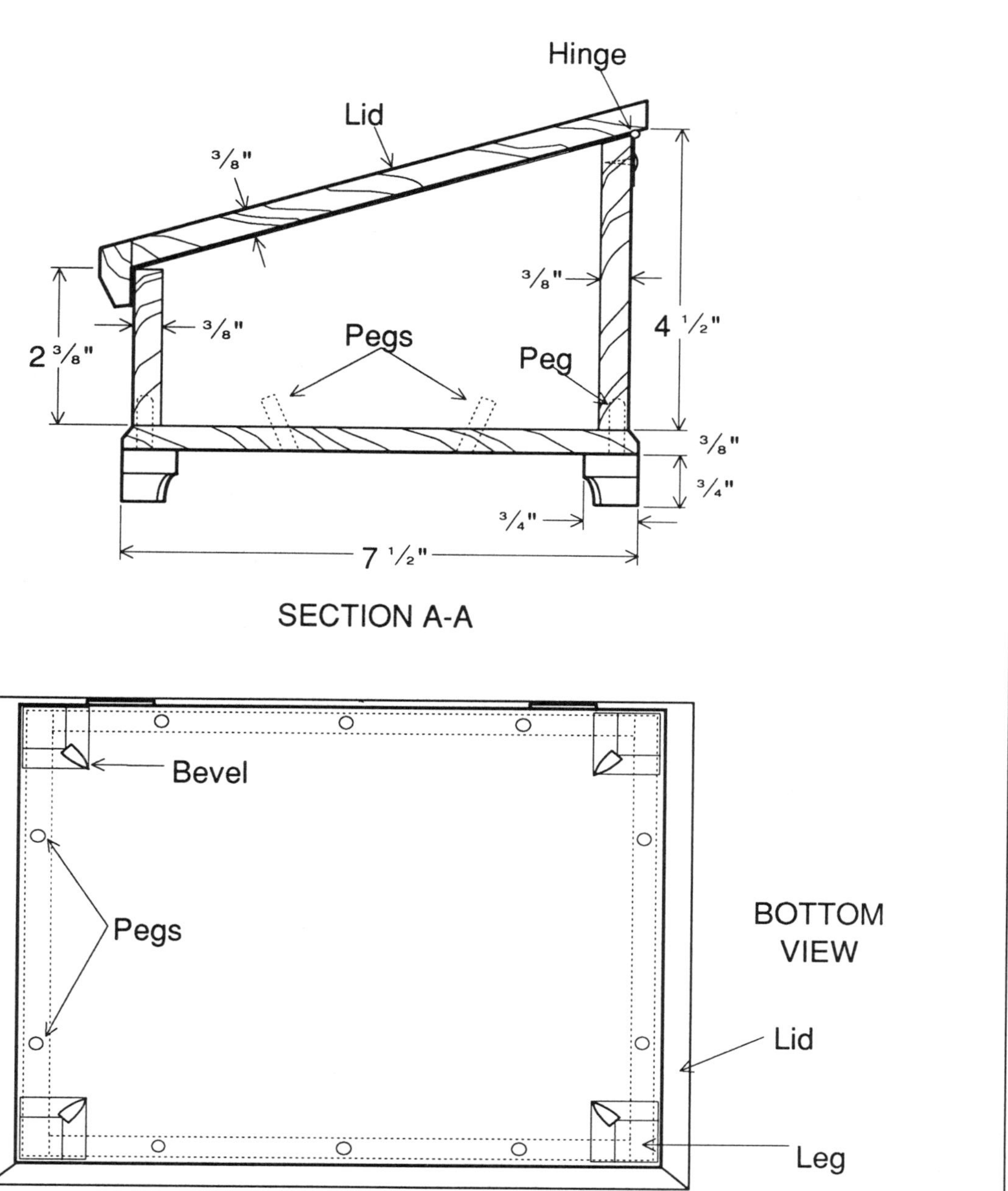
Hinge
Lid
3/8"
3/8"
3/8"
2 3/8"
Pegs
Peg
4 1/2"
3/8"
3/4"
3/4"
7 1/2"
SECTION A-A
Bevel
Pegs
BOTTOM VIEW
Lid
Leg

INSTRUCTIONS

Medium level of difficulty

Use pine, and, if you wish, oak, to make this box. Plane the sides (oak in the original), down to a thickness of ⅜″. Attach them with dovetails (see Introduction, joint #8).

For the bottom, plane pine to a thickness of ⅜″. The bottom will extend approximately ⅛″ past the sides all the way around. Bevel the edge on top. Fasten the bottom with wooden dowels. Drill the holes for the pegs obliquely up into the side pieces.

Cut feet for the box as shown, and fasten them with glued wooden dowels.

Use pine for the lid of the box, and plane it to a ⅜″ thickness. Plane edge strips for the three sides of the lid down to ½″ × ⅞″, and bevel them on the undersides. Fasten the edge strips on their sides by extending the lid piece to two 1½″-wide through tenons, which then butt against the edge strips. Fasten them with wooden dowels through the tenons. Fasten the strip on the front edge with wooden dowels. Drill the holes for the dowels straight into the lid piece. The lid of the box has mitred corners. In other respects the lid has the same design as the Chest which follows.

Fasten the hinges with nails or screws to the back of the box and the underside of the lid. The box may be made without a lock.

If you wish, you can paint this box with thin linseed oil paint to bring out the wood grain. Use a brown, such as burnt umber or burnt sienna.

CHEST

This small blue-and-red-painted chest from Södermanland is dated 1805. Chests or boxes of this type were used to store personal items. The so-called "sweetheart boxes" or "bride boxes" were particularly carefully made and decorated.

Despite the solid design with dovetailed sides, the lid held together by edge strips, and the interior compartment, this chest was undoubtedly made by a home woodworker. No particular difficulties should present themselves when making it. Hinges, locks, keys, and keyhole plate are another matter; in the past they would have been ordered from the village blacksmith. It is possible to find some of these fittings in antique shops. Otherwise you will have to be content with newly made iron fittings.

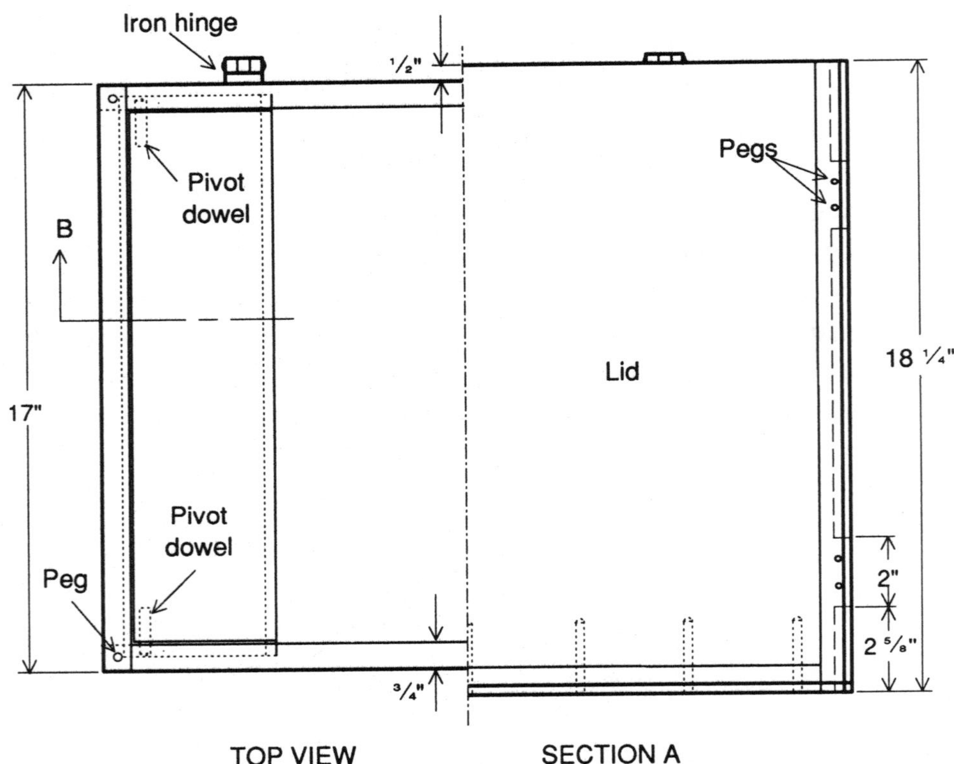

3/16" = 1
0 1 2 3 4 5 6 7 8 9 10 11 12 13 14 15 16

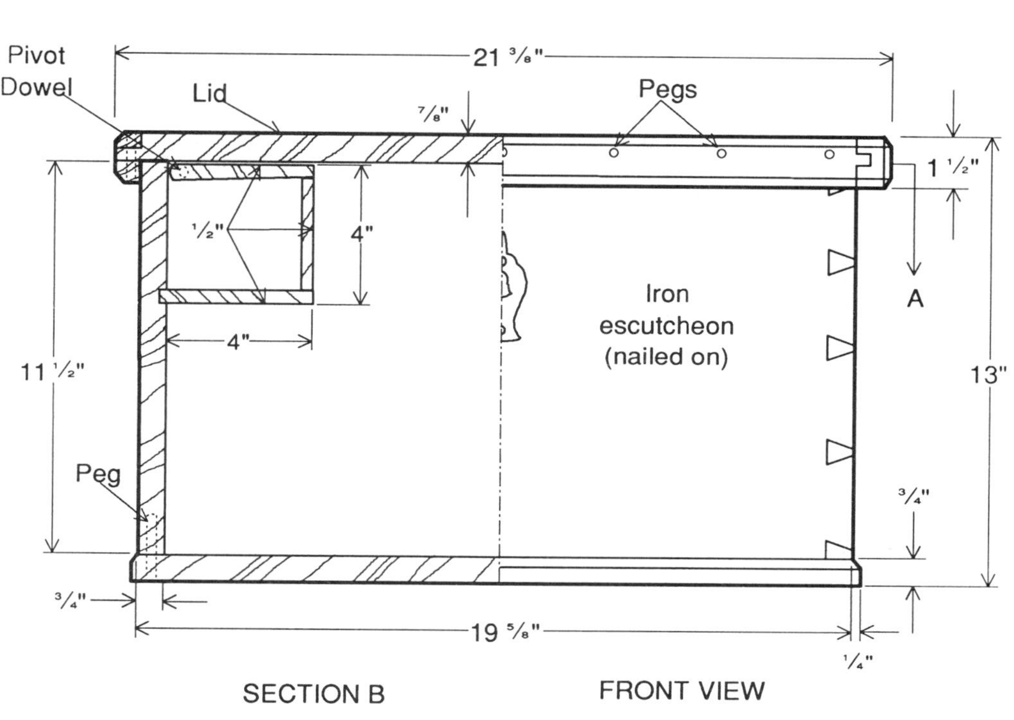

Pivot Dowel
Lid
21 3/8"
Pegs
7/8"
1 1/2"
1/2"
4"
4"
A
Iron escutcheon (nailed on)
11 1/2"
13"
Peg
3/4"
3/4"
19 5/8"
1/4"
SECTION B
FRONT VIEW

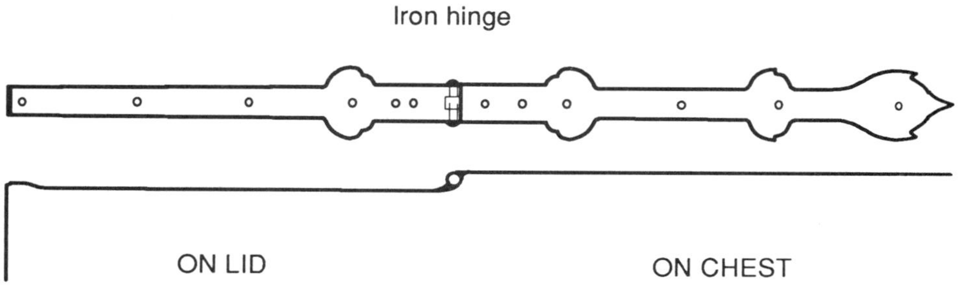

Iron hinge
ON LID
ON CHEST

INSTRUCTIONS

Fairly difficult to make

Use pine to make this chest. Plane the sides to a thickness of ¾″. Put them together with through dovetails (see Introduction, joint #8). Lock the joint from the top with a wooden dowel.

Plane the bottom to a thickness of ¾″. It should extend approximately ¼″ beyond the sides all the way around. Bevel the top of the edge. Fasten the bottom with wooden dowels. Drill the holes for them obliquely up into the side pieces.

Fasten the bottom and sides of the interior compartment with a ¼″ × ½″ rabbet (joint #1). Fasten the lid with tenons which are carved from the lid material, the same as in the preceding Jewelry Box.

The lid of the chest should be ⅞″ thick. The edge strips for the three sides should be planed to ¾″ × 1½″ and beveled. Rabbet the short ends of the lid (joint #6) to fit into the mortise in the edge strips. Fix these edge strips in place by extending the rabbet of the lid piece to 2″ wide tenons. These fit through the mortises on the edge strips and are locked in place at the tenons by wooden dowels. Fasten the strip at the front edge with wooden dowels and drill holes for them obliquely into the lid piece.

The hinges on the original chest are hand-forged and fastened with forged spikes on the back side of the chest and the underside of the lid.

The chest is painted blue (Prussian blue) with linseed oil paint. The chest's dovetail joints as well as the edge strips and corners of the lid, are painted red (red oxide).

HANGING CABINET

This small peasant cabinet from the beginning or middle of the 19th century was intended to be hung on a wall. The original imitation woodgrain painting and marbling in reddish-brown, blue, and red is well preserved. As is usual in cabinets from the 18th and 19th centuries the door is attached by pin hinges which are nailed to its top and bottom edges.

This cabinet was probably made by a home woodworker on a small farm in Dalsland or northern Bohuslän. No lock was needed, and the molding strips and the frame around the door panel were made with only a couple of molding planes. Hanging cabinets of this type have also been found in other parts of Sweden, with variations in the shape and painted colors.

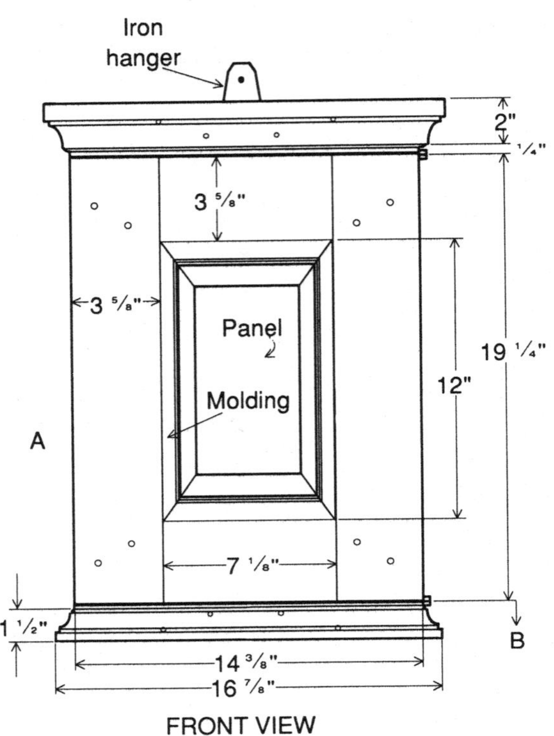

FRONT VIEW

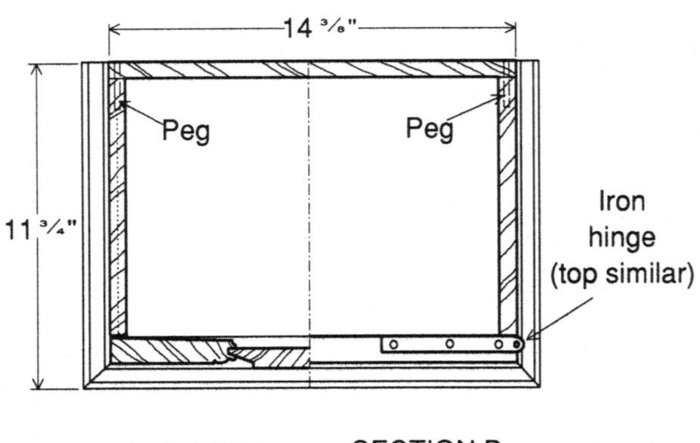

SECTION A SECTION B

1/8" = 1

0 2 4 6 8 10 12 14 16 18 20 22 24

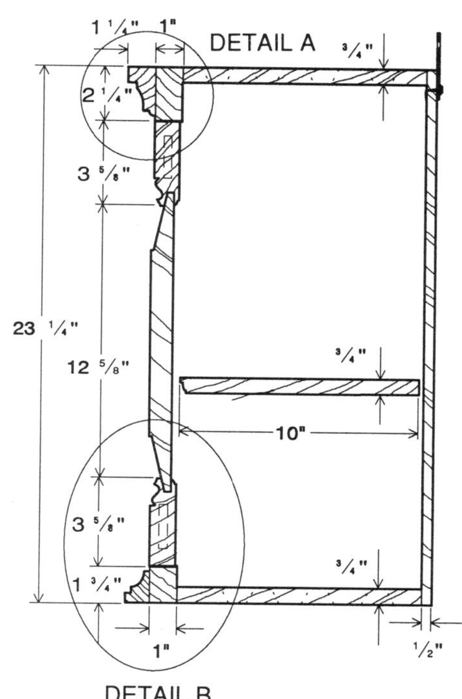

INSTRUCTIONS

Fairly difficult to make

Use pine to make this cabinet. Plane the boards for the body, the bottom, the top, and the sides down to ¾″. Fasten them at the corners with through dovetails (see Introduction, joint #8). Notice that the dovetail joints are made in the cabinet's sides, since it is intended to hang on the wall. Plane the interior shelf to a thickness of ¾″. Fasten it in place with a ½″ rabbet (joint #1), ending approximately ½″ inside the front edge of the shelf. Make a ½″ thick back for the body and fasten it with wooden dowels. Fasten crown moldings to the top and bottom of the body with wooden dowels. Drill holes for them obliquely into the top, bottom, and side pieces.

Make the door frame 1″ thick, with a mold on the inside edge. Put it together with through tenons (joint #9) and lock them with 1/4″ diameter dowels. Bevel the 3/4″ thick door panel with a rabbet plane and place it into the groove of the frame without gluing it. Use pin hinges and fasten them with nails or screws into the trim above and below the door frame. These hinges can be found in hardware stores.

The original cabinet has only one hanger fitting, but we recommend you use two for added safety. The hanger fittings are made of two pieces of forged steel plate fastened with nails or screws into the back of the cabinet. The original cabinet has never had a lock.

The original cabinet was painted with linseed oil paint. The cabinet body crown moldings, and the door frame are a burnt umber brown. The door panel is bluish-green (Prussian blue), and the molded part of the door frame is painted bright red (red oxide).

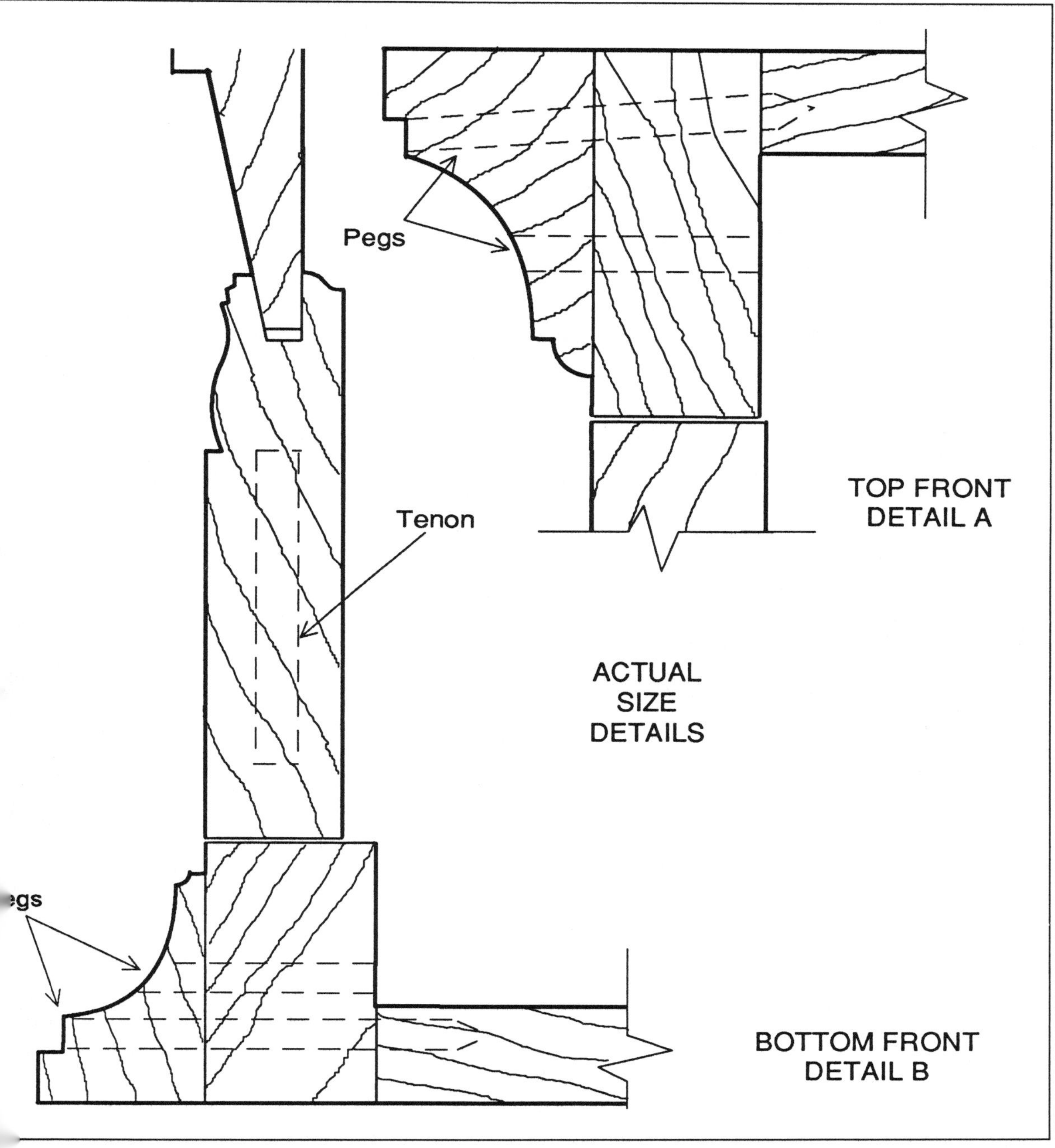
Pegs
Tenon
TOP FRONT
DETAIL A
ACTUAL
SIZE
DETAILS
egs
BOTTOM FRONT
DETAIL B

TRESTLE TABLE

Trestle tables of unpainted pine are examples of a very ancient and basic type of furniture. They have been found in every setting, from aristocratic homes to small farms and crofts, where they survived into the 19th century.

The legs consist of two trestles connected by a crossbar, which is joined through the uprights of the trestles and locked on the outside with wedges.

This tabletop, which is somewhat more recent than the trestles, is made of several planks which are glued together. It is lent additional solidity by strips which are slot dovetailed into the underside and locked with pins through the upper braces of the trestles.

The table was not painted.

INSTRUCTIONS

Medium level of difficulty

Use pine to make this table. Connect the parts of the trestles, uprights and braces by making ½″ × 2½″ tenons on both ends of the uprights, and cutting mortises through both the upper and lower braces. Lock each tenon with two wooden dowels. Make mortises in the uprights for the connecting crossbar, and mortise each end for wedges. To save a little material you can make the ornamented ends of the crossbar separately and glue them on.

Continued on page 148

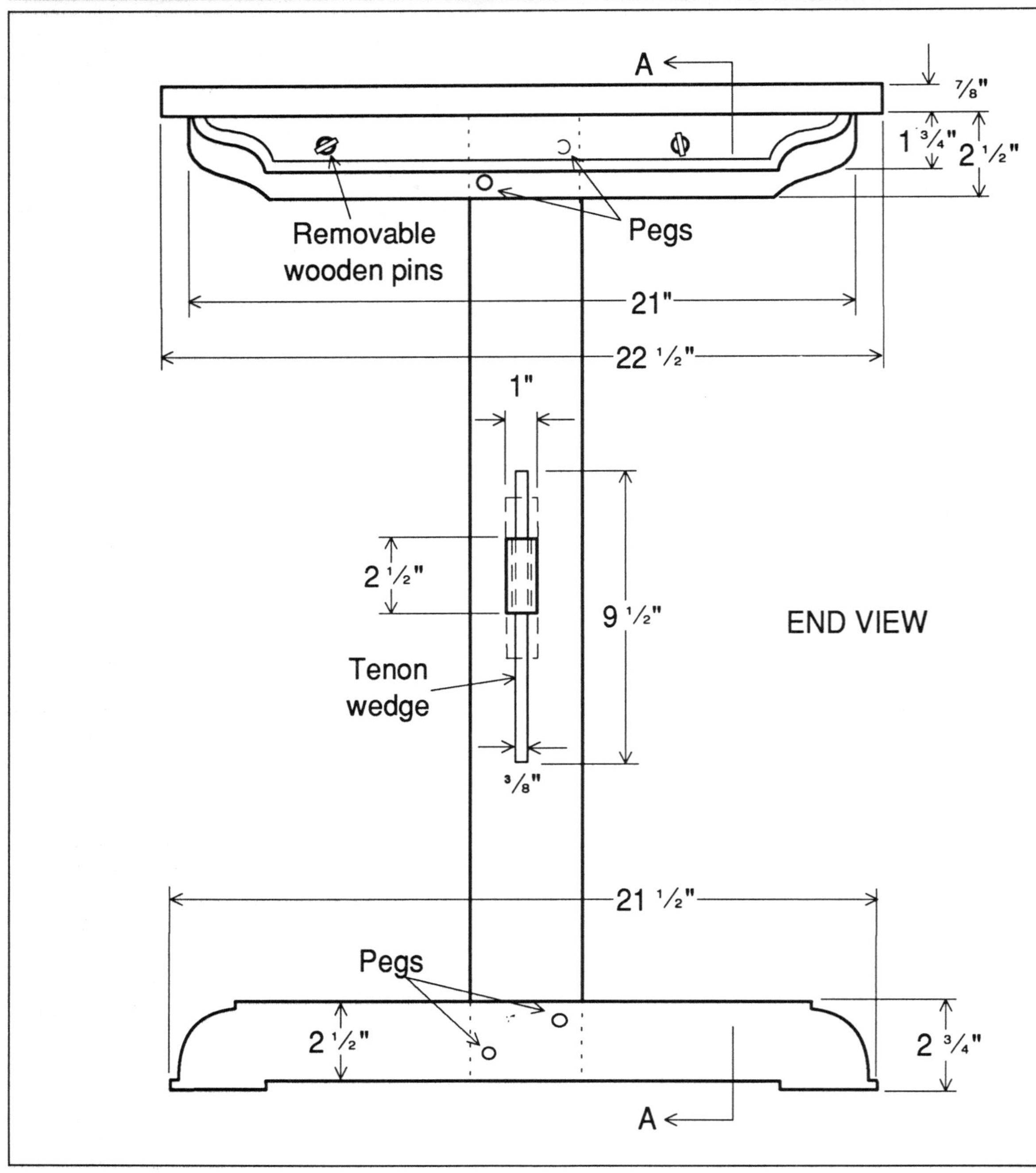
A
7/8"
1 3/4"
2 1/2"
Removable
wooden pins
Pegs
21"
22 1/2"
1"
2 1/2"
9 1/2"
END VIEW
Tenon
wedge
3/8"
21 1/2"
Pegs
2 1/2"
2 3/4"
A
0 1 2 3 4 5 6 7 8 9 10 11 12 13 14 15 16
3/16" = 1

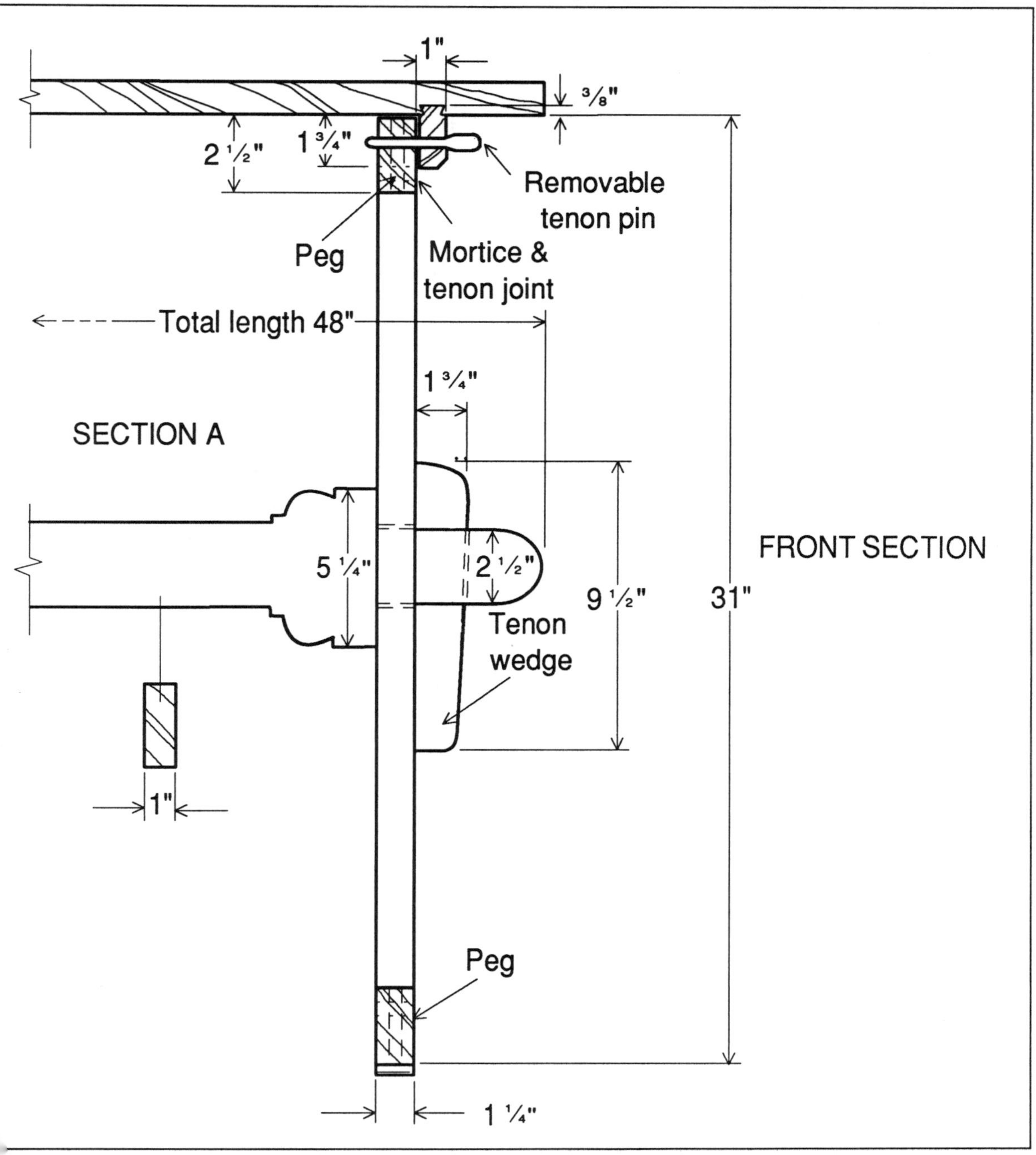
1"
3/8"
2 1/2"
1 3/4"
Removable
tenon pin
Peg
Mortice &
tenon joint
Total length 48"
1 3/4"
SECTION A
FRONT SECTION
5 1/4"
2 1/2"
9 1/2"
31"
Tenon
wedge
1"
Peg
1 1/4"

Make the tabletop with 7/8″ thick boards, holding them together with two slot dovetailed rails (see Introduction, joint #4). Drill holes for four wooden pins through the rails and the upper braces of the trestles.

This table does not require finishing. If you do want to treat the surface, you can brush it with a mixture of linseed oil and turpentine. Alternatively, it can be painted a reddish-brown color—a mixture of English red and burnt sienna.

BENCH

This bench, which can be used outdoors, is now in Älvrosgården at the Skansen exhibit. In contrast to the simplest sitting benches, which consist of a plank loosely laid on two trestles, this bench has a seat plank in which two pairs of contoured and somewhat extended legs are joined with wedged tenons. The simple design, without edging or reinforcements between the legs, requires solid dimensions for the bench to hold.

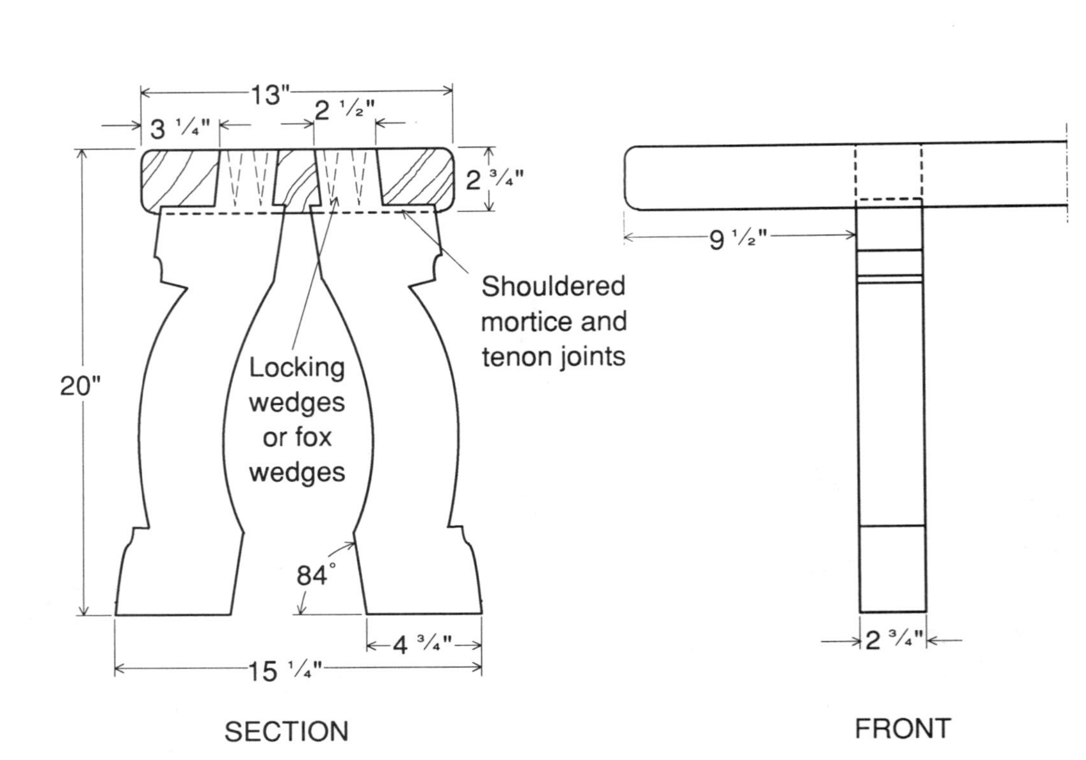

INSTRUCTIONS

Fairly easy to make

Use pine or oak to make this bench. It can be made any length up to 8 feet. Plane the seat from one massive plank to a thickness of 2¾". Cut rectangular mortises in the seat, and wedge the tenons of the legs with heavy wedges. Note that the wedges must be placed perpendicular to the grain of the seat plank, or else it may crack.

To finish it, brush the bench with a mixture of linseed oil and turpentine.

1/8" = 1

0 2 4 6 8 10 12 14 16 18 20 22 24

GATE-LEGGED TABLE

This pine gate-legged table from the Gustavian period is the most common 18th century table design. During the 19th century it was found frequently in peasant and working-class homes.

The base consists of four legs held together by frames and foot rails. A fold-out gate is fastened to each side.

The tabletop consists of a narrow center piece and two fold-out rectangular leaves, articulated with two forged hinges riveted to the underside. The leaves consist of several planks glued together, attached by two transverse bracing strips on the underside. Tabletop panels and strips are

A newly made unfinished gate-legged table. Note the large bolt heads on the top side of the leaves and center panel, which fasten the hinges on the underside.

fastened with a slot dovetail. No glue or nails were used, giving the various parts freedom of movement in changing humidity. For this reason, along with the select, properly dried pine, these old tabletops have not warped or cracked.

The tabletop's narrow center piece is fastened to the base with carved

The newly made table is shown here with one panel raised.

wooden pegs through holes drilled in the bracing strips and in the short frame pieces of the base.

One detail that gives the table a timeless, well-made appearance is the rounded moldings on the long sides of the center piece and the corresponding concave shape of the drop leaves. The original table's grayish-white linseed oil paint is preserved, though worn.

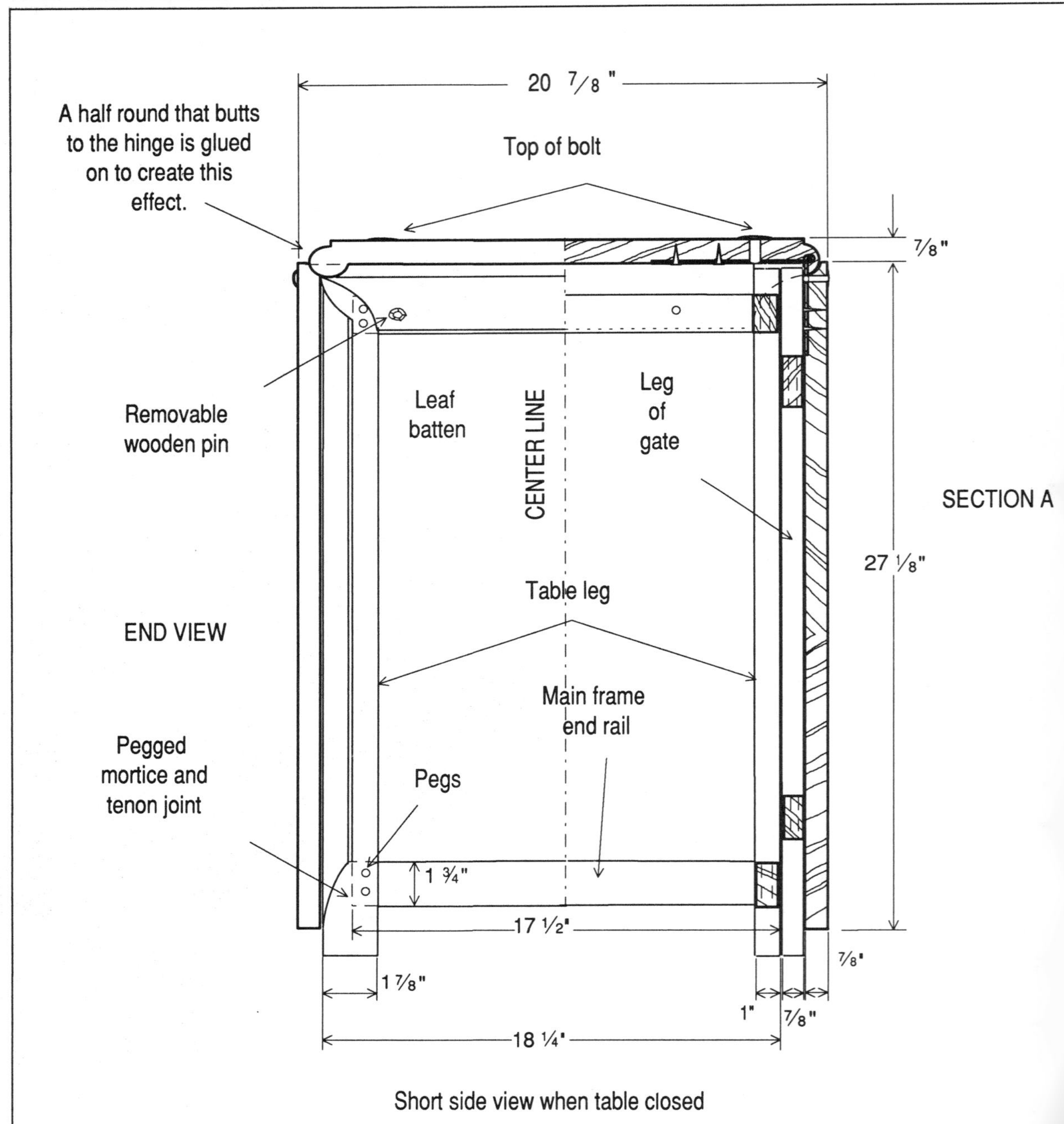

Short side view when table closed

1/8" = 1

0 2 4 6 8 10 12 14 16 18 20 22 24

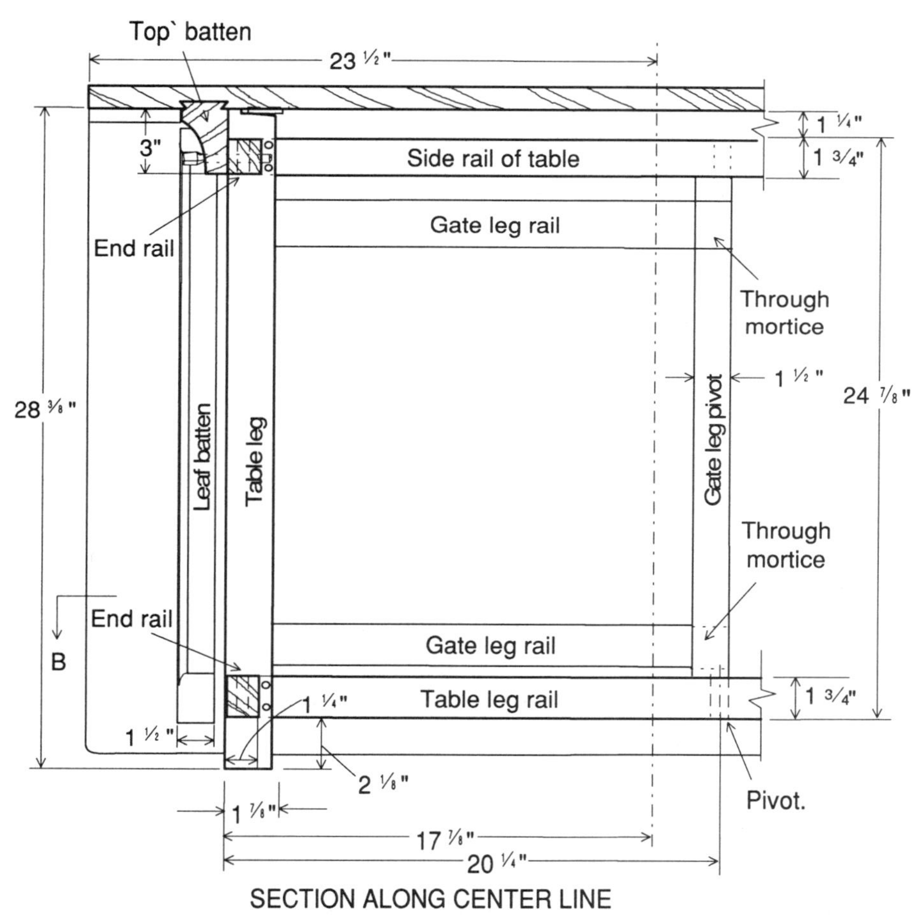

SECTION ALONG CENTER LINE

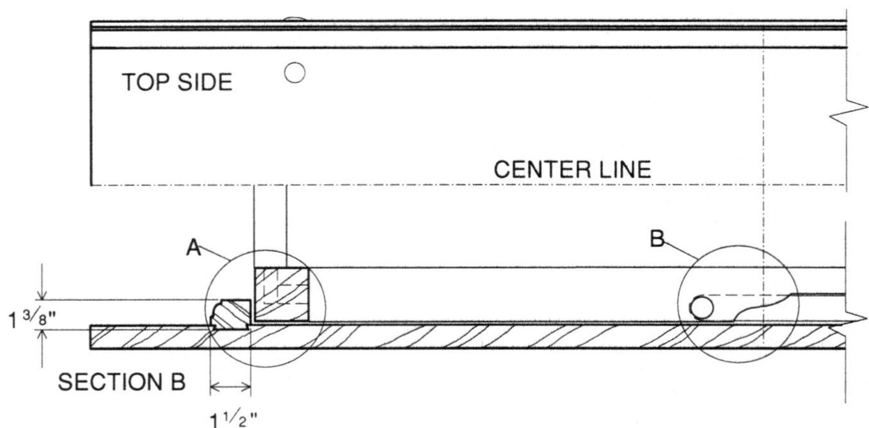

INSTRUCTIONS

Difficult to make

Use pine to make this table. Plane the legs, frame, and gates to the dimensions shown in the drawing. In the long frame members make ⅜″ holes for the round tenons that support the gates. Lock the tenons of the frame members in the legs with double wooden dowels. For the panels, use massive, wide boards, reinforced and held together with 3″ wide bracing strips. Note that the bracing strips should not be glued along their entire length, but only for a short area at the hinge side.

The rounded molding along the hinge side of the panels may be difficult for many people to make. It is easier to leave the edges straight—also a common variation. Note how the hinge is placed for the first case. If you make the simpler version, be sure to turn the hinge so that the fulcrum will be on the underside of the panel.

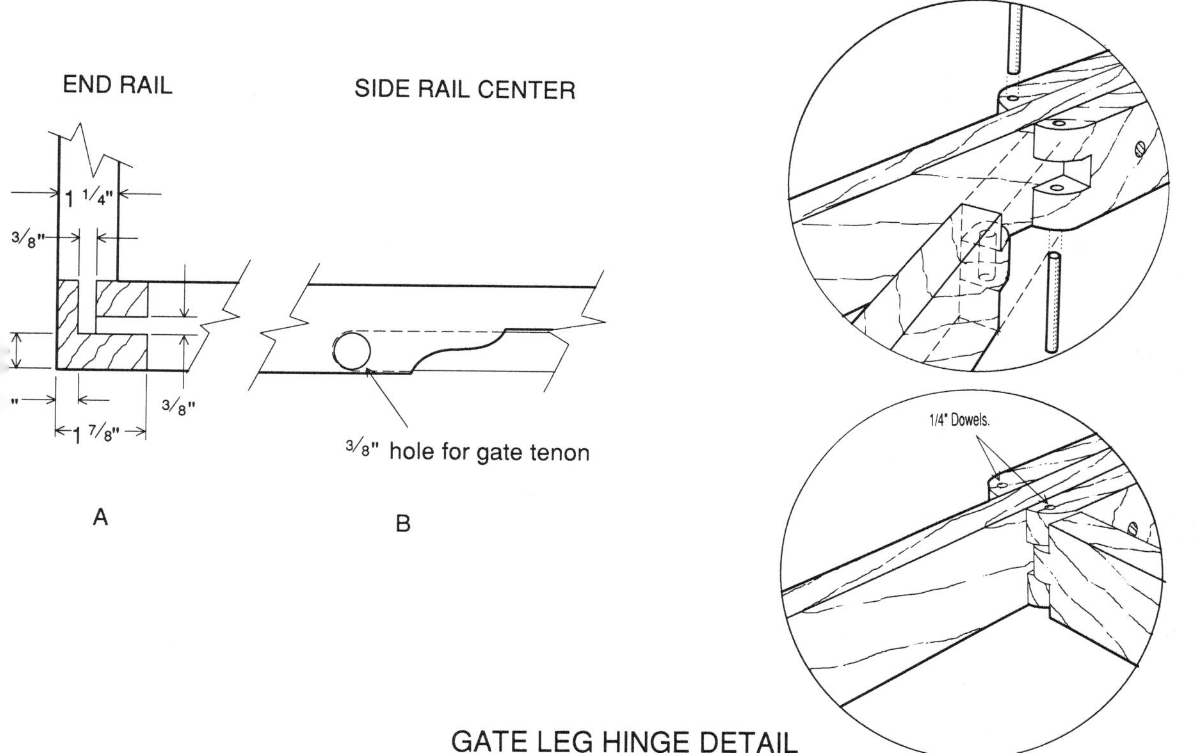

GATE LEG HINGE DETAIL

Make holes in the center panel's bracing strips for the wooden dowels which lock the panel to the base of the table. Fasten the hinges with bolts which are riveted on the underside (or use screws instead). Of course, ordinary hinges from the hardware store may also be used.

To match the original, paint the table with linseed oil paint in a light gray color—a mixture of zinc white and burnt green earth.

The photo on page 159 shows a variation of the gate-legged table, with semicircular drop leaves and double gates as supports. In contrast to the first table, this one has straight planks instead of four legs and so takes up even less space when it is folded up.

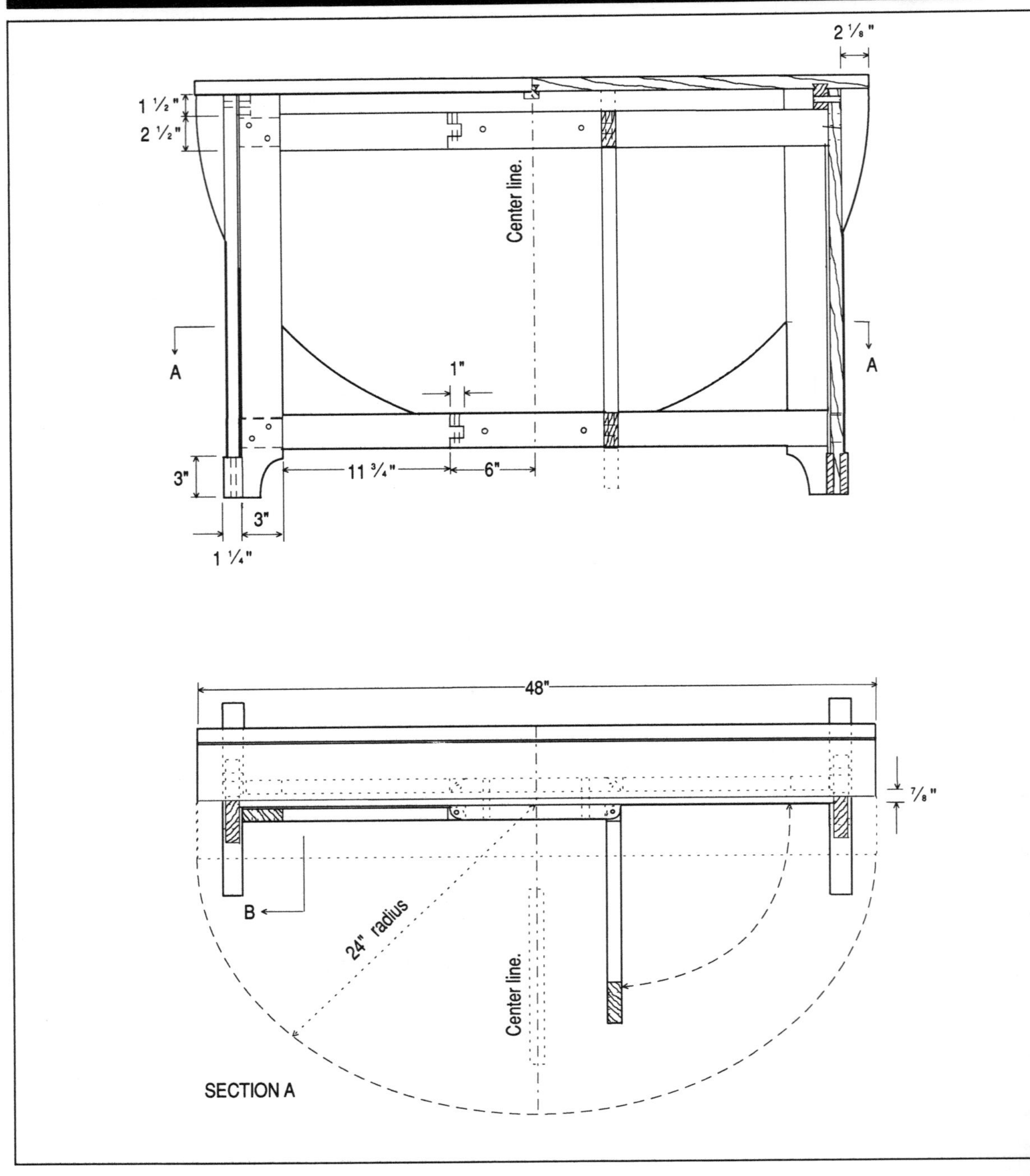

2 1/8"
1 1/2"
2 1/2"
Center line.
A
A
1"
3"
11 3/4"
6"
3"
1 1/4"
48"
7/8"
B
24" radius
Center line.
SECTION A
0 2 4 6 8 10 12 14 16 18 20 22 24

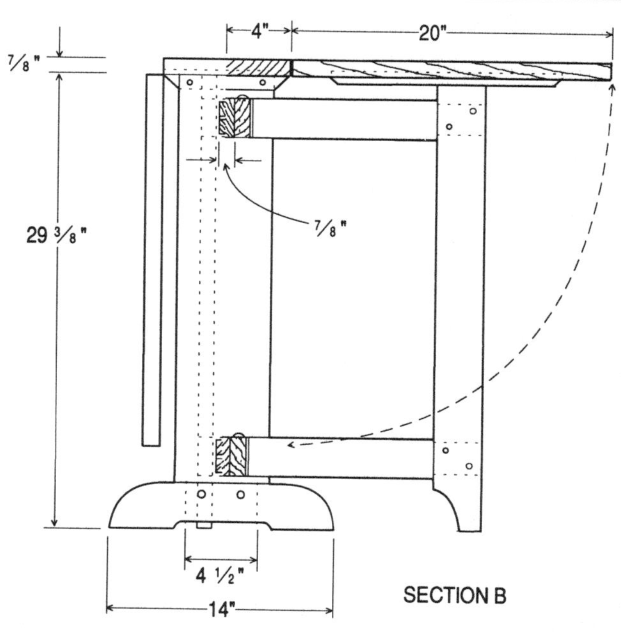
4"
20"
7/8"
29 3/8"
7/8"
4 1/2"
14"
SECTION B

CHAIR

This alder chair is from the latter part of the 18th century, and is known as a "pin chair" or "ladder-backed chair." This type of chair has been called southern European, since from the start of the 18th century it was found primarily in France, but it was also found in England, from where it spread to North America. In Sweden this type of chair has also been named for Östervåla in Uppland, where it was made during the 18th and 19th centuries.

This model shows the usual design, with straight, turned legs. The back legs continue up as back uprights, into which horizontal, bentwood back pieces are inserted, the upper somewhat broader than the lower ones. Apparently these back pieces, if they were thin, obtained their curved shape by being steamed, bent, and fitted in between the back uprights, at the same time as the leg crossbars were inserted to prevent the back pieces from straightening out. Thicker back pieces were sawed to their curved shape. Bars, crossbars, and frame members were held together and locked with pegs.

The wooden seat is loosely dropped into a rabbet in the heavy frame members. In Sweden the seat may also consist of a frame, with a saddle, and horsehair stuffing. In the rest of Europe and in America this type of chair usually has a woven raffia seat or one with a similar fibrous material, which does not require actual frame members.

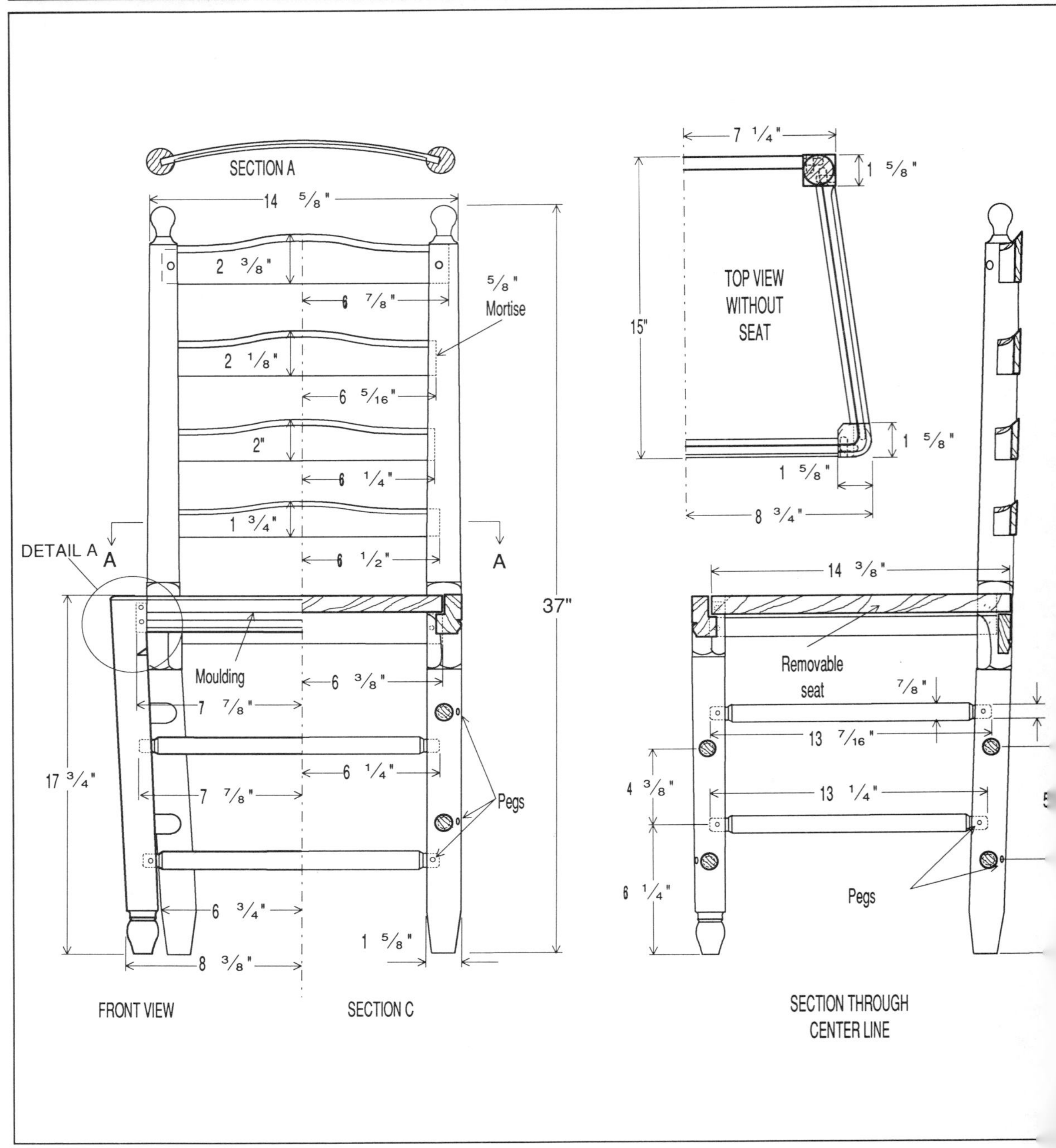

1/8" = 1
0 2 4 6 8 10 12 14 16 18 20 22 24

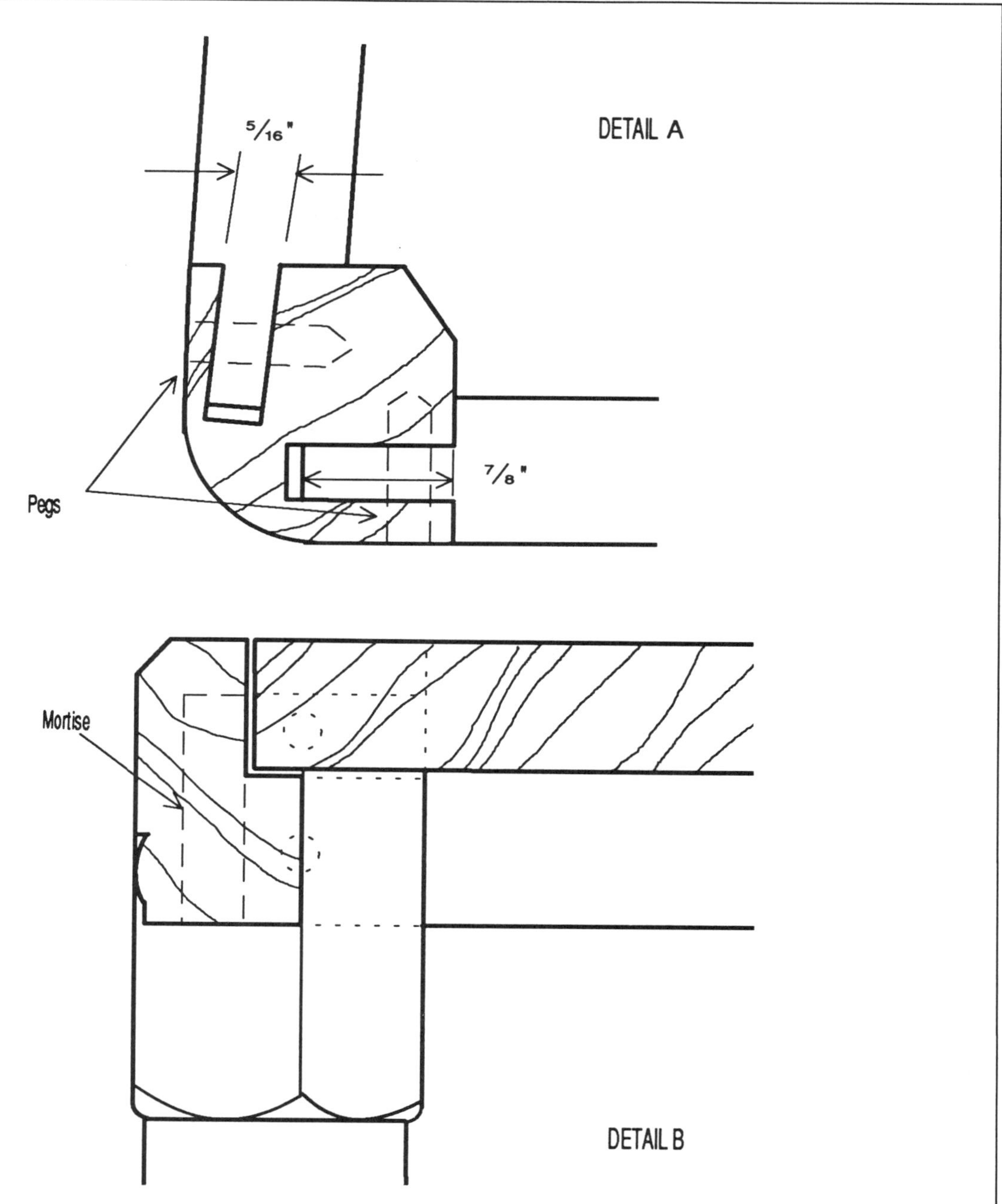
DETAIL A
5/16"
7/8"
Pegs
Mortise
DETAIL B

INSTRUCTIONS

Fairly difficult to make

Use hardwood to make this chair.

Turn the front legs to a 1⅝″ diameter. Also turn the back legs to a 1⅝″ diameter, but gradually reduce them above the frame, so that the back uprights are 1½″ in diameter at the transition to the knob.

Cut the front and side frames 1¾″ high and 1″ thick. Mold and rabbet them (see Introduction, joint #6) for the seat, as shown in the diagram. Cut the back frame 1⅝″ high and ⅝″ thick, and also mold the lower edge.

The front legs should be vertical, the seat horizontal, and the angle of the back uprights in relation to the seat should be 1.5°. In the original the back legs are also inclined to the side. The distance to the center is ⅝″ greater at the top than at the bottom.

Turn the leg crossbars to a ⅞″ diameter. Turn them at their ends so that the tenons are ⅝″ in diameter.

Cut the back crossbars to their curved shape. Note that not all the tenons have to be secured with wooden dowels. Secure the tenons of the back frame with one wooden dowel, and the tenons of the side frames with two wooden dowels.

For the seat use a single ¾″ thick wooden slab. This will lie loosely in the rabbet of the frame. Or you can secure it with ¼″ wooden dowels, through holes drilled horizontally through the frame and into the seat. Alternatively, you can place the seat on a retaining frame, as in the seat of the Footstool which follows.

The original chair was painted with an opaque light gray oil paint. To match it start with zinc white tinted with burnt green earth and add lampblack.

These two armchairs and footstool combine to form a reclining seat. They are in Finland, in Sveaborg's museum, outside Helsinki.

ARMCHAIR

This is one of the simplest versions of the "Gripsholm fauteuil" type of armchair. It is named after similar chairs which stand in the Cavalier Wing of Gripsholm castle. It is made with a straight back, so that the back legs continue as the back uprights. The turned armrests also have turned supports instead of the curved, sculpted ones that are most common. The three horizontal slats on the back, which have no bevel on the upper edge, are also fairly roughly made. They were originally steam bent, but have straightened again with time.

This armchair was made of alder, and originally painted with a greenish-blue oil paint. It once had a solid stuffing, but from the start it probably had a loose cushion resting directly on webbing nailed to the top edge of the frame.

This Gripsholm fauteuil is one of the oldest examples preserved from the 18th century. A similar armchair, with a solid woven grass seat, was used in the simpler rooms of Drottningholm castle during the middle and latter part of the 18th century. One example, also with turned armrests and armrest supports, has been preserved in Sweden's Royal Collection. Another is now in the children's room in the Skogaholm manor house at the Skansen exhibit.

This version of the armchair shows an arrangement with loose cushions on the back and seat. Note the stuffed and upholstered bead along the top edge of the frame, which holds the seat cushion in place.

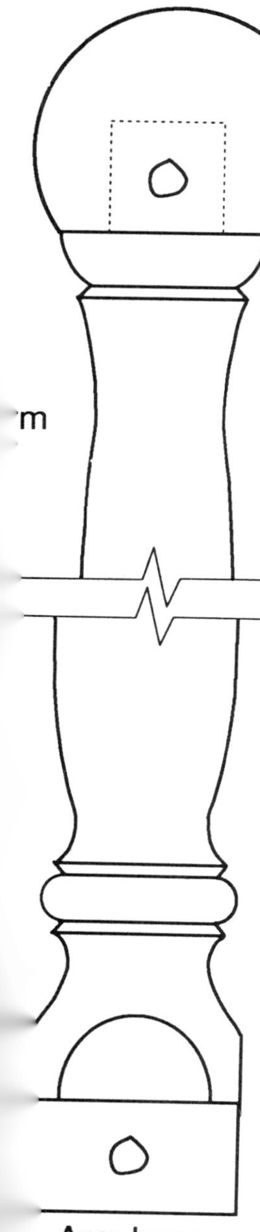

Arm base

INSTRUCTIONS

Fairly difficult to make

Use hardwood to make this armchair, except for the back uprights, which are made of pine. Turn the front legs to a 1 3/4″ diameter at the frame, and taper them slightly downward to a 1 5/8″ diameter at the feet. Turn the back legs to a 1 1/2″ diameter below the frame. Above the frame, reduce the diameter slightly, so that it is 1 7/16″ at the knob.

Plane all the rails to 1 1/4″ × 2 1/4″. Turn the leg rungs to a 1″ diameter at their thickest point, and turn the tenons to an 11/16″ diameter with a 1″ depth.

In contrast to the chair, the armchair's back slats are planed very thin, approximately 1/4″, steamed, and then bent in between the back uprights into 3/4″ deep mortises. (Alternatively, you can saw the slats out of 1 1/2″ thick stock.)

Turn both the armrests to a diameter of 1 13/16″. Then plane them off on the top and bottom to a thickness of 1 1/4″, and scoop them out on the top to make room for the horsehair stuffing. Secure all tenons with 3/16″ wooden dowels. Also secure the tenons of the frame in the back legs with two 3/16″ wooden dowels.

The armchair should be provided with loose cushions for the seat and back. The original seat cushion rests on hemp webbing covered with a piece of linen, both stretched and nailed to the frame.

You can paint this armchair with light blue linseed oil paint—a mixture of zinc white and cobalt blue or Prussian blue.

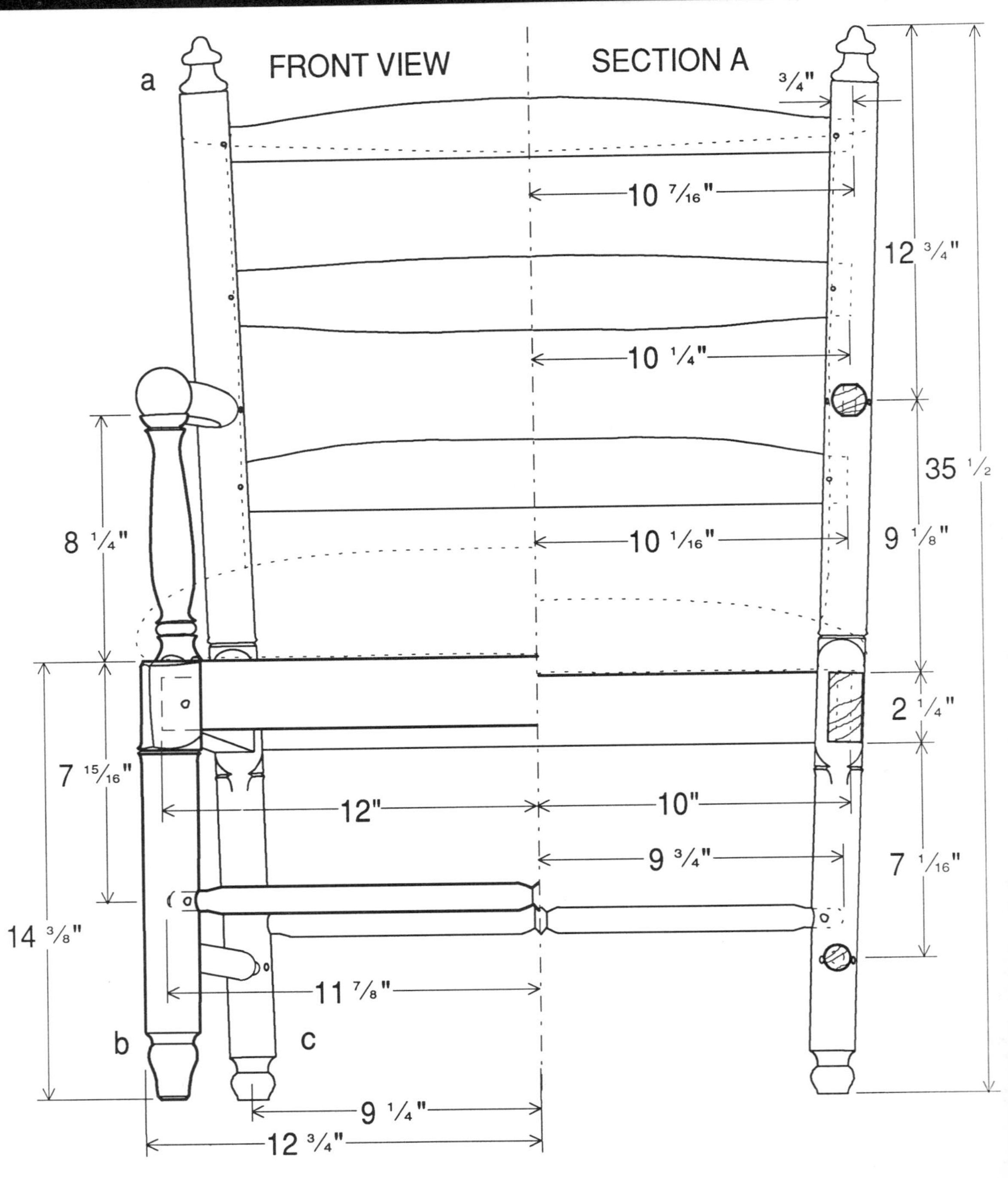
FRONT VIEW
SECTION A
a
b
c
3/4"
10 7/16"
12 3/4"
10 1/4"
35 1/2
8 1/4"
10 1/16"
9 1/8"
2 1/4"
7 15/16"
12"
10"
9 3/4"
7 1/16"
14 3/8"
11 7/8"
9 1/4"
12 3/4"
3/16" = 1
0 1 2 3 4 5 6 7 8 9 10 11 12 13 14 15 16

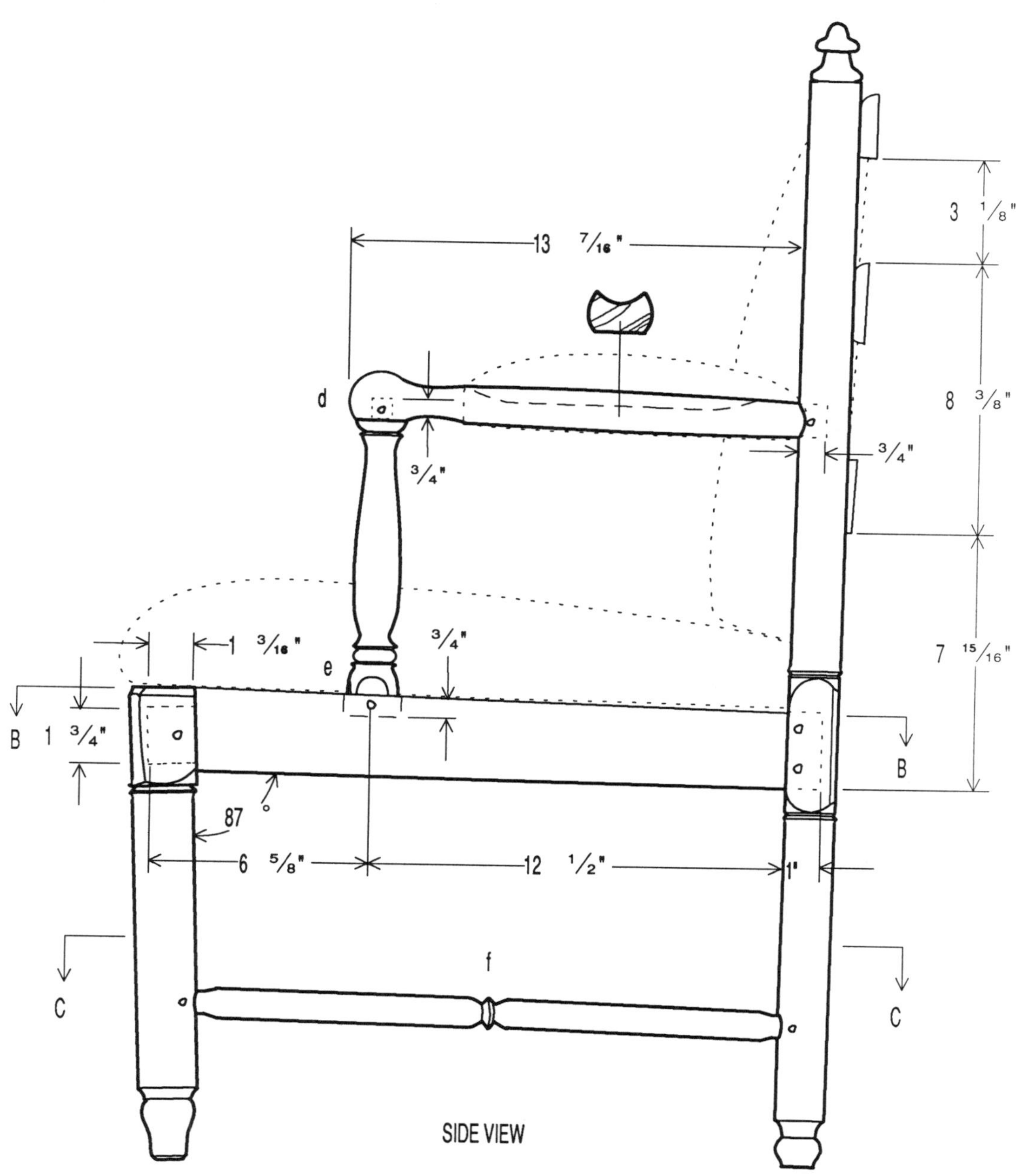

SIDE VIEW

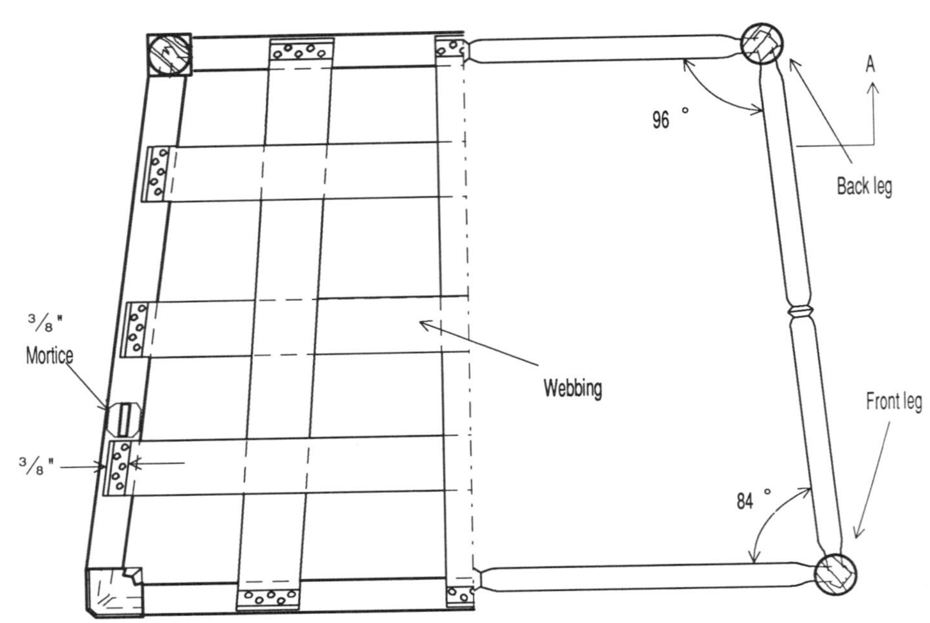

A
96 °
Back leg
3/8"
Mortice
Webbing
Front leg
3/8"
84 °
SECTION B
SECTION C

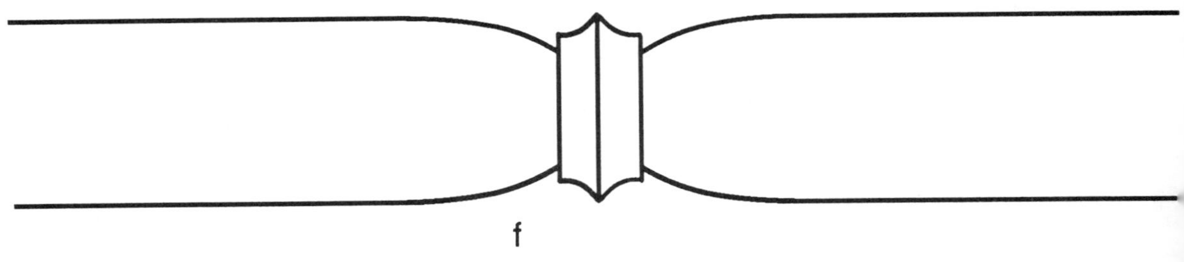

f

Leg rung

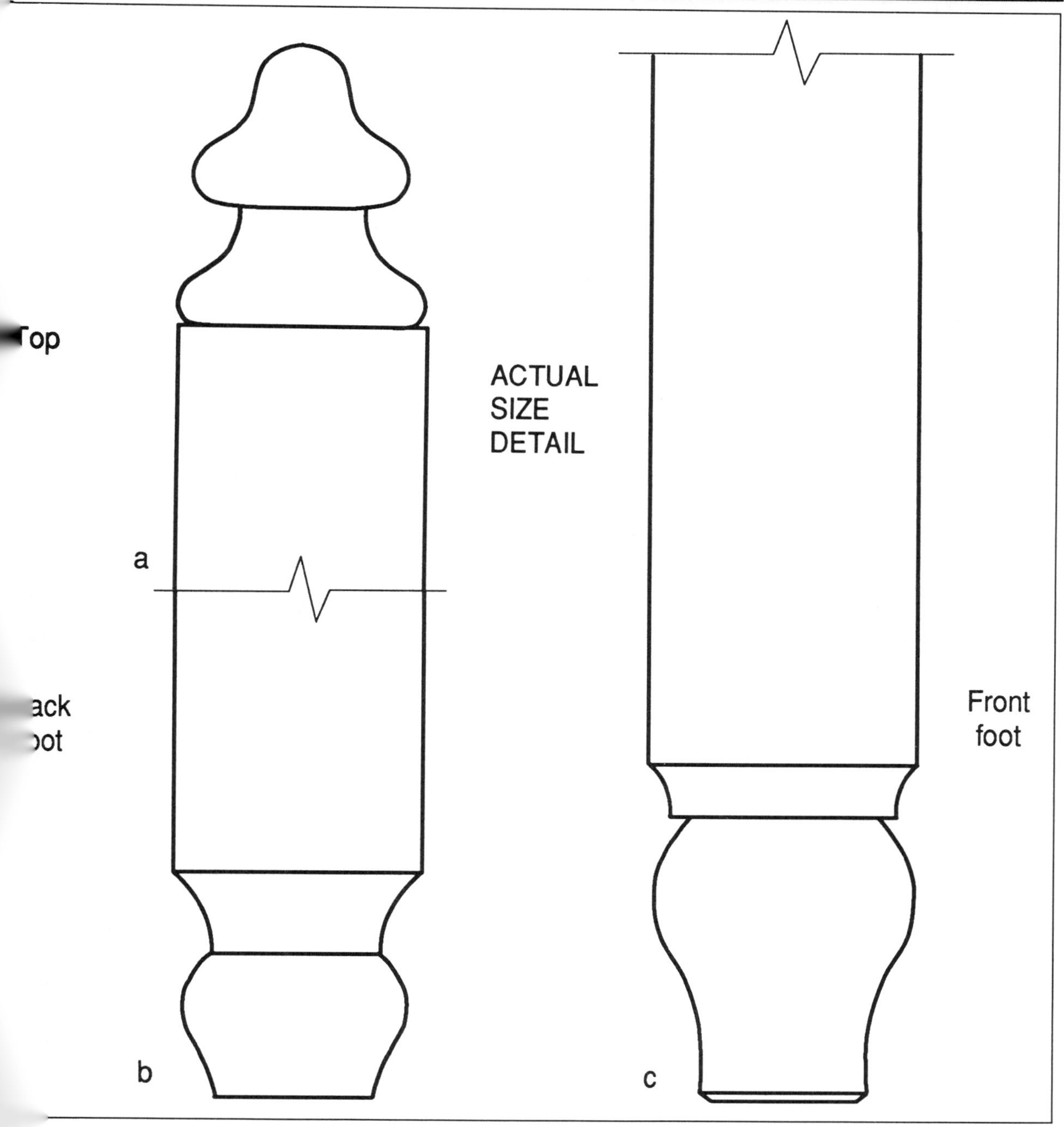

Top

a

ACTUAL SIZE DETAIL

Back foot

b

Front foot

c

FOOTSTOOL

This footstool follows the traditional Gripsholm style, and is from a manor house in northern Uppland, from the latter part of the 18th century. The material is alder. The straight-turned legs with pear-shaped feet are connected by heavy frame members with a rabbeted edge to house the loose seat frame. The round, slightly spool-shaped leg rungs were placed at different heights so as not to weaken the legs unnecessarily. The model ob-

viously matches and belongs with the Gripsholm armchair. At one time somewhat larger footstools of the same type were also used to extend armchairs, or to combine two armchairs into a reclining seat. (See the photo on page 165.)

The photo below shows a newly made footstool before painting and without the seat.

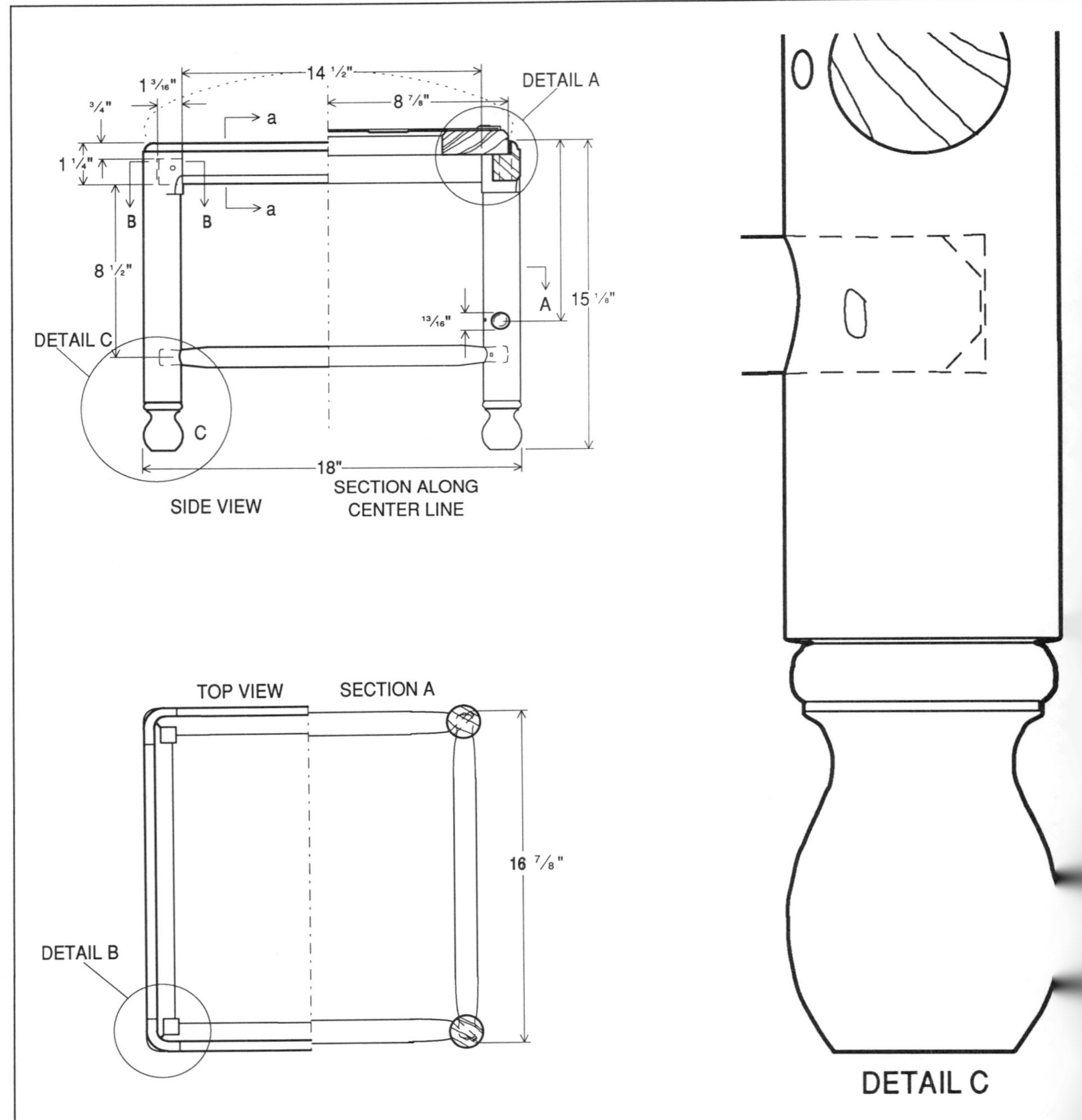

1/8" = 1
0 2 4 6 8 10 12 14 16 18 20 22 24

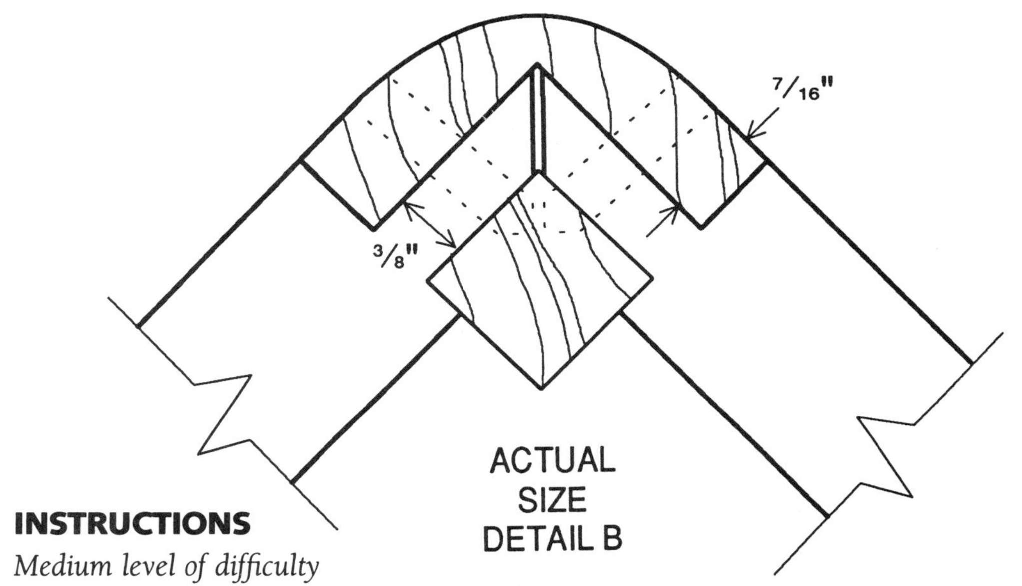

INSTRUCTIONS

Medium level of difficulty

Use hardwood to make this footstool. Turn the legs to a diameter of 1 11/16". Leave their upper parts square until you have assembled the footstool. Then round off the four outer corners with a plane. Note that in the original, about 4" of the upper part of the legs became slightly tapered inward as a result.

Make the frame members 2" high and 1 3/4" thick. Bevel and mold them, and rabbet them (see Introduction, joint #6) out for the seat frame. Turn the leg rungs to a 1" diameter. Taper them at the ends so that the tenons are 13/16" in diameter. Secure the tenons of the frame members and the rungs with 1/4" wooden dowels.

This footstool has a loose, stuffed seat. Cut 3" × 1 13/16" pine for the seat frame. The original stuffing, of horsehair and cotton wadding, rests on hemp webbing, covered with linen.

You can paint the footstool with linseed oil paint in a reddish-brown, imitation mahogany color (burnt sienna and red oxide or English red), or in pearl-gray (zinc white and burnt green earth).

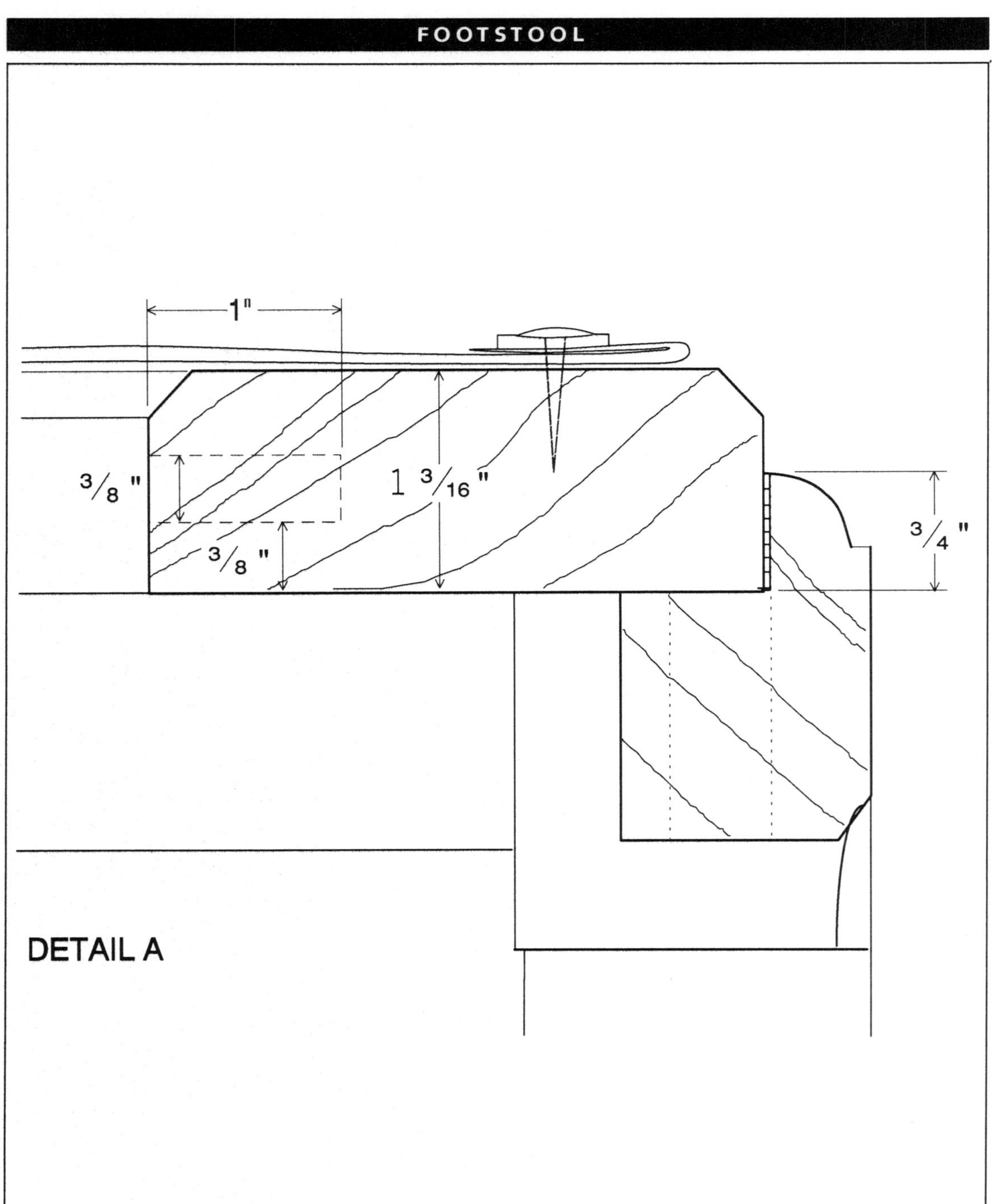
1"
3/8 "
1 3/16 "
3/8 "
3/4 "
DETAIL A

SMALL SIDE TABLE

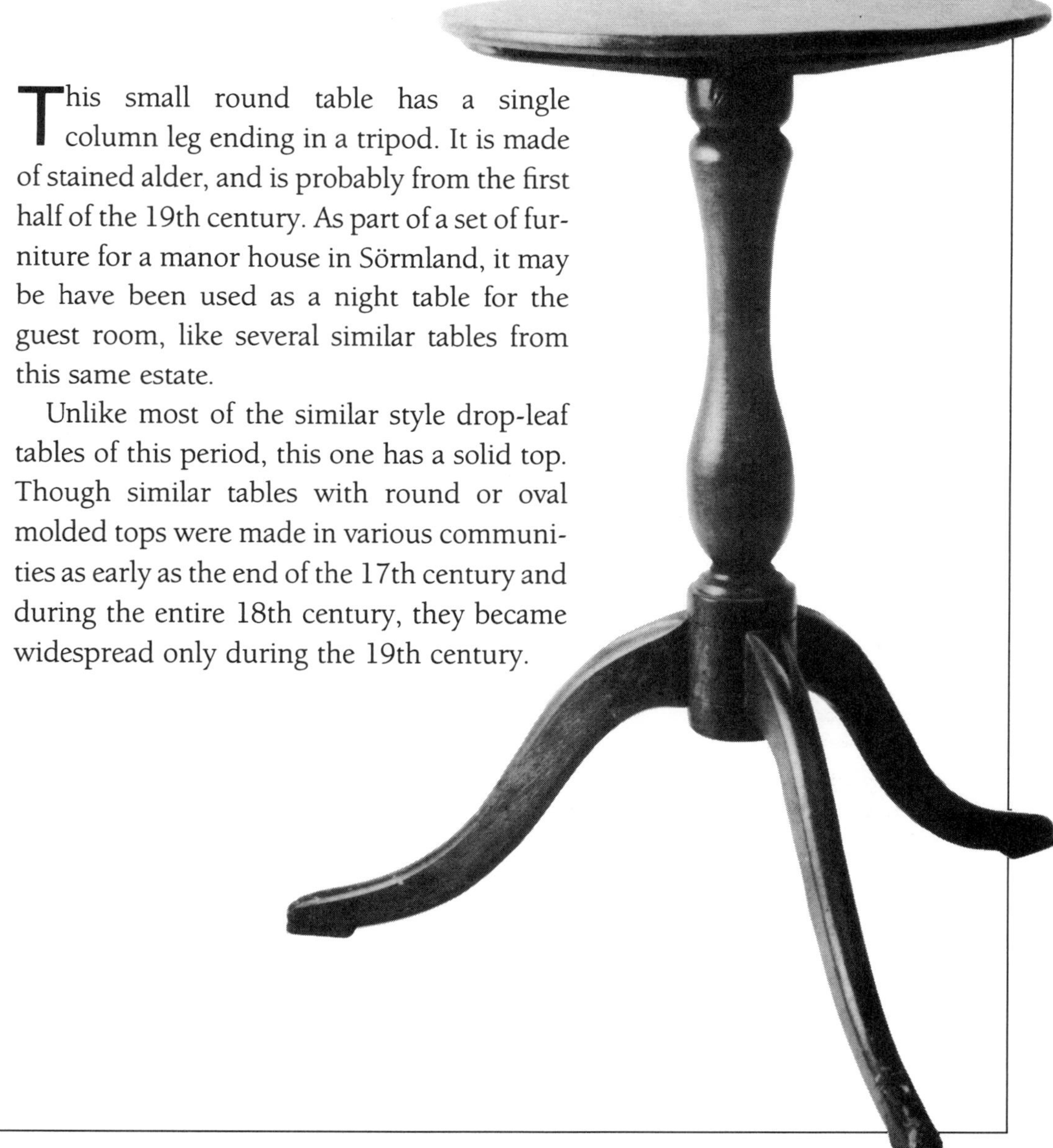

This small round table has a single column leg ending in a tripod. It is made of stained alder, and is probably from the first half of the 19th century. As part of a set of furniture for a manor house in Sörmland, it may be have been used as a night table for the guest room, like several similar tables from this same estate.

Unlike most of the similar style drop-leaf tables of this period, this one has a solid top. Though similar tables with round or oval molded tops were made in various communities as early as the end of the 17th century and during the entire 18th century, they became widespread only during the 19th century.

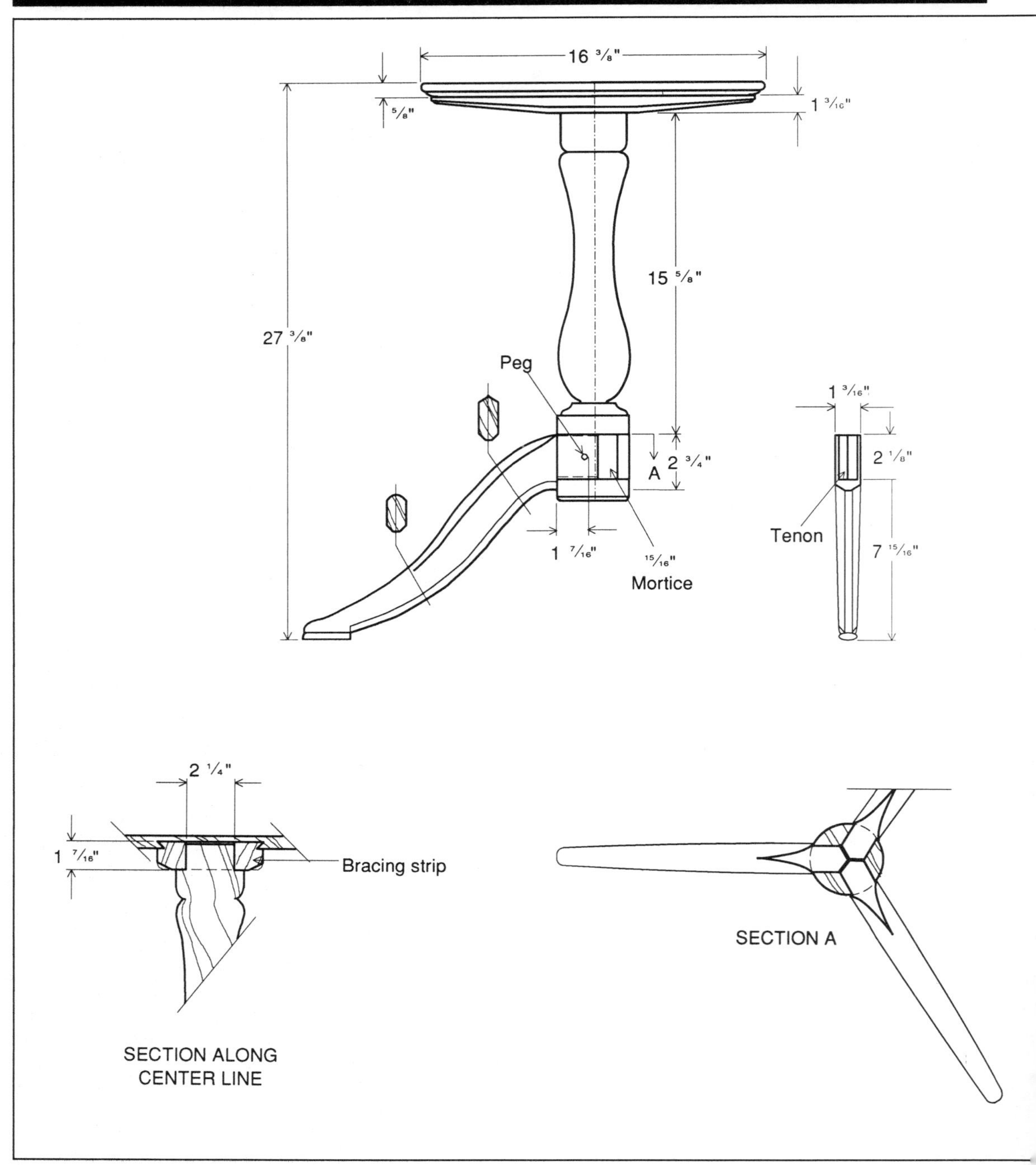

SECTION ALONG CENTER LINE

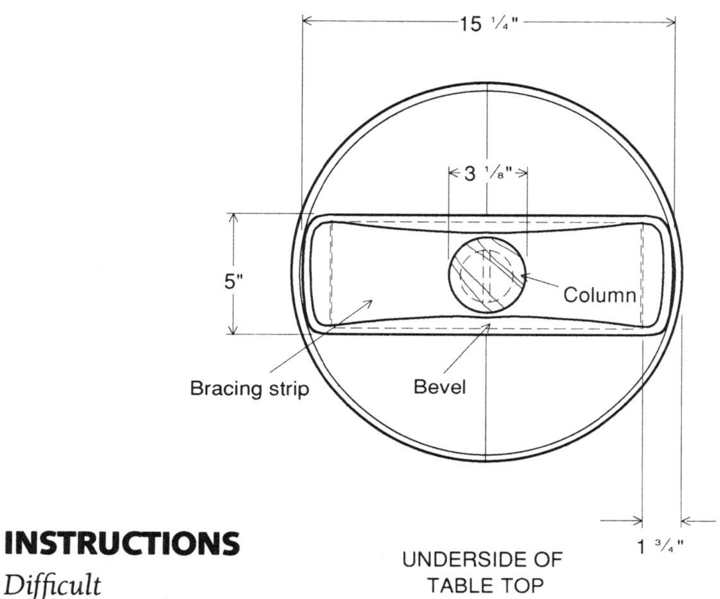

INSTRUCTIONS

Difficult

Use hardwood to make this table. Turn the column in one piece. Secure the tenons of the feet in the pillar with 3⁄16″ wooden dowels. At the top of the column fasten the bracing piece to hold together and reinforce the tabletop. Attach the bracing piece with a through wedged tenon from the column.

Make the tabletop of two halves, planed to a 5⁄8″ thickness. Bevel the lower edge. Make a dovetailed groove in the underside of the two halves of the tabletop, having it end about 1¾″ from the outer edge of the tabletop. Slip the tabletop halves onto the bracing strip, one from each side, and glue the joint between the two halves. But note that the bracing strip, which is dovetailed to the tabletop, must not be glued to it, to keep the top from splitting.

The original table's color is not known. It was later painted a reddish-brown (burnt sienna) with linseed oil paint to imitate mahogany. The table may also be oil-varnished after painting.

TRESTLE BED

This bed of gray-painted pine is now in the Garvargården at the Skansen exhibit. Its simple but ingenious design comes from an ancient Swedish tradition. It consists of four posts connected by side pieces. These are made of straight planks with tenons that are wedged into the headboard and footboard. Beds of this simple type were used during the 18th and 19th centuries in inns and in the servants' rooms of castles and manor houses. Some similar beds are preserved in the servants' quarters of the Cavalier Wing of Gripsholm castle.

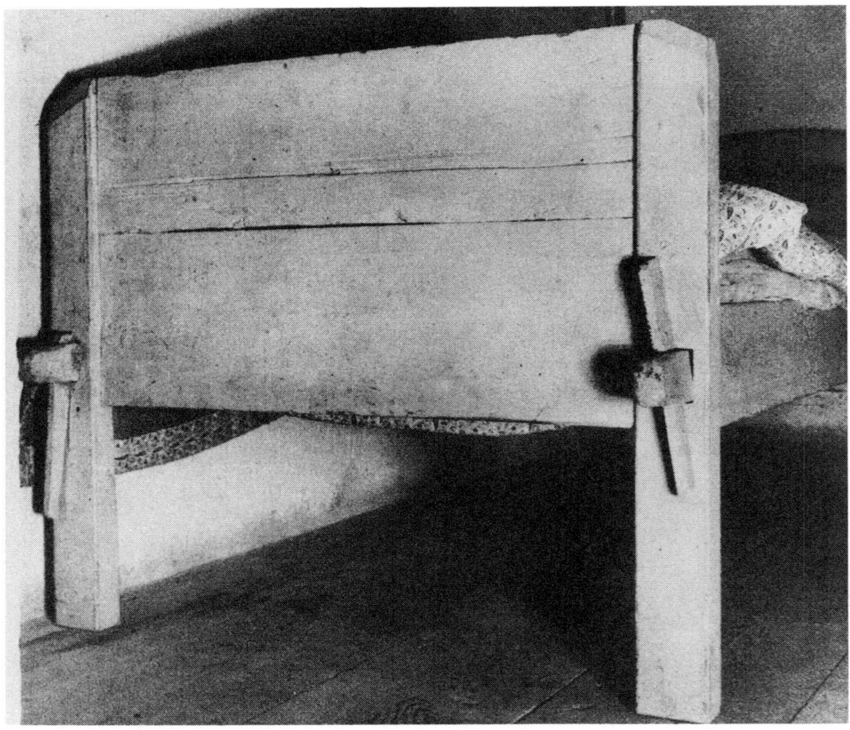

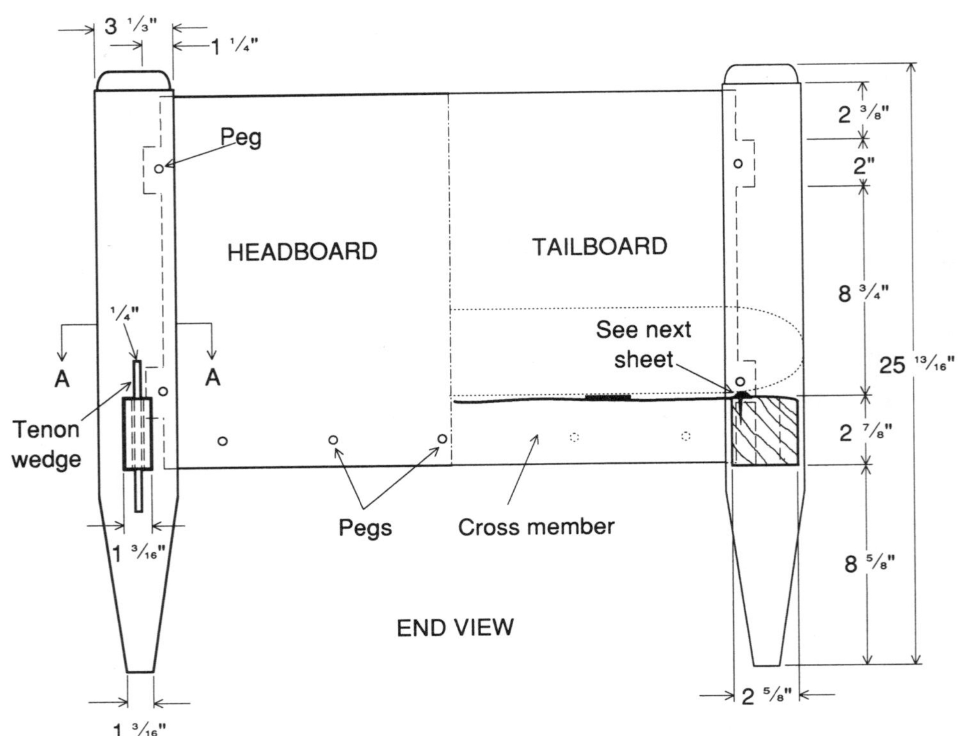

INSTRUCTIONS

Medium level of difficulty

Use pine to make this bed. The inside length of the original bed is 71 13/16″, but you can adjust the length to suit your own requirements. To make the ends, rabbet (see Introduction, joint #6) a ⅝″ thick pine slab into the legs and secure them with wooden dowels. On the bottom of the inside of the bed ends, fasten a cross member with ⅜″ wooden dowels. Webbing is then stretched and nailed to the cross member. Make rectangular holes in the legs for the connecting long sides. Make a rabbet in the sides for the webbing across the bottom of the bed. Secure the long sides to the bed ends by

1/8" = 1
0 2 4 6 8 10 12 14 16 18 20 22 24

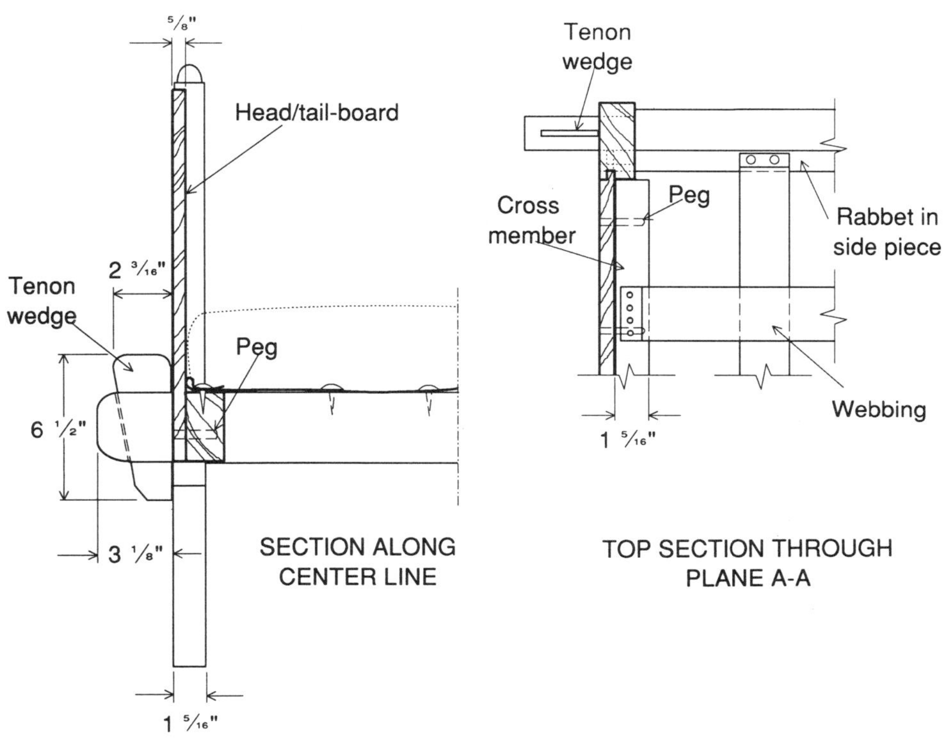

wedges. The width of the wedges in the original can be reduced by approximately 13⁄16″. This will reduce the risk of splitting the projecting tenons of the long sides.

The bottom of the original bed is made of hemp webbing nailed into the rabbet of the long sides and the cross member of the bed ends. Of course, you can use a modern variation, such as a sheet of plywood or loose wooden slats.

The original bed is painted with light gray linseed oil paint—a mixture of zinc white and burnt green earth.